Gumption & Grit

WOMEN OF THE CARIBOO CHILCOTIN

EXTRAORDINARY WOMEN VOL. 1

Gumption & Grit

WOMEN OF THE CARIBOO CHILCOTIN

CAITLIN PRESS

Collected by the Contact Women's Group Society

— EDITED BY SAGE BIRCHWATER —

with Gloria Atamanenko, Pam Mahon and Karen Thompson

Caitlin Press Inc.
8100 Alderwood Road
Halfmoon Bay, BC, V0N 1Y1
604 885 9194
1 877 964 4953
WWW.CAITLIN-PRESS.COM

Design by Michelle Winegar
Printed in Canada

All images courtesy the author or their family unless otherwise noted. We acknowledge the *Williams Lake Tribune* for their generous permission to use their photos in the *Casual Country* stories.

Caitlin Press Inc. acknowledges financial support from the Government of Canada through the Book Publishing Industry Development Program and the Canada Council for the Arts, and from the Province of British Columbia through the British Columbia Arts Council and the Book Publisher's Tax Credit.

Canada Council **Conseil des Arts**
for the Arts **du Canada**

BRITISH COLUMBIA
ARTS COUNCIL
Supported by the Province of British Columbia

LIBRARY AND ARCHIVES CANADA CATALOGUING IN PUBLICATION

Gumption & grit : extraordinary women of the Cariboo Chilcotin /
edited by Sage Birchwater.

Thirty-five stories chosen from those collected in 2002
by the Women's Contact Society of Williams Lake.
ISBN 978-1-894759-37-3

1. Women pioneers--British Columbia--Cariboo Region--Biography.
2. Women pioneers--British Columbia--Chilcotin River Region--Biography.
3. Frontier and pioneer life--British Columbia--Cariboo Region. 4. Frontier
and pioneer life--British Columbia--Chilcotin River Region. 5. Cariboo Region
(B.C.)--Biography. 6. Chilcotin River Region (B.C.)--Biography. I. Birchwater, Sage II. Women's
Contact Society (Williams Lake, B.C.) III. Title: Gumption and grit.

FC3845.C3Z48 2009   971.1'75030922
C2009-905593-7

This book is dedicated to the courageous women of the Cariboo Chilcotin.

Table of Contents

Coming Later: New Perspectives and Skills

Coping: Personal Adversities and Finding Strength

Foreword

DIANA FRENCH

I t isn't known who, but some Caucasian women who arrived in the Cariboo Chilcotin in the late nineteenth century brought lilac bushes with them. The hardy plant was shared with others, and to this day the bushes can be found all over the place, on ranches, in villages, and beside abandoned cabins in the bush.

I like to think the lilac symbolizes what women have brought to the Cariboo Chilcotin: strength and a touch of beauty.

At one time they used to say the Cariboo Chilcotin, with its vast wilderness, wild and rugged landscape, capricious and sometimes vicious weather, was a man's country. The inference was that women simply weren't up to coping with it on their own. Cowboys would boast that in this particular wild west, men were men and the women were proud of it. There was also a saying that the Cariboo Chilcotin was a great country for men but hell on women and horses.

Both statements were true, up to a point; the point being, there was never a shortage of hardy women standing shoulder to shoulder with the men, willing and able to face whatever the country or fate threw at them.

The stories of some of these women have been gathered into *Gumption & Grit: Women of the Cariboo Chilcotin*, which is part of a new series called *Extraordinary Women*. I personally haven't met many women in the Cariboo Chilcotin who weren't extraordinary in some way or another. Most don't know they are anything special. They just do what they have to do, with love and humour, be it making a home in the wilderness, writing books, breaking horses, trying to make the world a better place, raising families, raising spectacular gardens, putting their lives back together after some disaster, sometimes all of the above.

As for grit and gumption, it took a good helping of both for women to leave the comfort of their homes and families to venture into unknown territory. Most found adventure, although it may not have been what they expected. Many stayed, married local men, and in most instances, lived happily ever after.

The women who came to the country with their husbands to start a new life, or a new job, had their own set of challenges.

It takes grit and gumption to deal with illness, or to overcome personal adversity, as some women have. Sometimes it takes grit and gumption simply to survive in tough circumstances, to cope with whatever comes along. While First Nations women and others born in the country didn't have to deal with culture shock, they had other issues to deal with.

The women portrayed in this book came from all walks of life. Each is unique. When their stories are put together they give a snapshot of life in the Cariboo Chilcotin from a woman's perspective.

The list of women who played significant roles in local history is endless. All of these women deserve to have their stories told. Hopefully the following editions of this new series will help complete the picture.

Introduction

BY GLORIA ATAMANENKO

Women of the Cariboo Chilcotin have always had the beauty of this region to cheer and inspire them, and the difficulties posed by great distances, isolation and climatic extremes to challenge their initiative and creativity. Secwepemc, Tsilhqot'in and Dakelh (Carrier) women lived here first. In the mid-nineteenth century, Caucasian women began to arrive, following in the footsteps of their men who began colonizing the region searching for trading opportunities, gold and land to settle. The coming of these newcomers brought some benefits for Aboriginal people, but also tragic consequences. The aftermath of this interface of cultures is still in the process of resolution and healing.

Aboriginal and European women had knowledge and skills from their own traditions which they shared with one another. This melding of wisdom and know-how now enriches our common heritage.

This project to collect women's stories in the Cariboo Chilcotin was initiated by Jenny DeReis, acting executive director for the Women's Contact Society in Williams Lake in 2004. She says the idea for the book occurred many years earlier when she was working in the field of violence against women, coordinating the first specialized victim assistance program in Prince George. "There was this group of us young, idealistic women determined to change the world and end sexism and violence against women," she says.

Then DeReis was confronted by a reporter who told her that young feminists didn't seem to know much about the history of older women and the barriers they overcame in male-dominated fields. "She suggested one day it would be nice if younger women could recognize and honour these older, retired women."

In June of 2005 the Women's Contact Society of Williams Lake hired Erinn Brown to collect stories from women about their experiences breaking into male-dominated fields and overcoming barriers because of gender or other discriminating factors.

Through newspaper and radio ads, Erinn put out a call for volunteers to tell their stories or write stories for those who didn't wish to write about themselves. In some cases she matched writers with the storytellers. As the stories flooded in the Contact Society began to realize that what they were receiving was an amazing collection of women's stories of diversity, challenge and courage. Erinn was encouraged to edit them for inclusion in a book, but at the end of the summer not all the stories had been collected and it was hoped the project would continue the following summer. Unfortunately funding to continue the project never materialized and the project sat dormant for three years.

In September 2008 representatives from the Contact Women's Group Society appealed to *Williams Lake Tribune* writers Sage Birchwater and Gaeil Farrar to edit the collected stories and prepare the material for publication. There were a little over twenty stories when Gaeil and Sage agreed to work with the project. Over the winter they added several more stories to the collection, some of which had previously been published in the newspaper or in the *Tribune*'s annual prize-winning supplement, *Casual Country*. The stories in the collection now number over forty.

When Caitlin Press publisher Vici Johnstone learned of the project, she expressed an interest in publishing the stories under the title *Gumption & Grit: Women of the Cariboo Chilcotin*. The stories in this book come from different time periods—from the late 1800s to the present day. These accounts reflect changing social conditions and needs. The necessity of making a living under difficult circumstances held opportunities for women to transcend traditional limitations on their roles and behaviours. In some women these challenges led to highly creative endeavors. Some of these stories offer a rare glimpse into their times. Other women struggled to undo the consequences of forced assimilation and dedicated their lives to help preserve linguistic and cultural heritage.

The Cariboo Chilcotin is essentially two vast regions bisected by the Fraser River. The women of this country have provided political leadership as First Nations chiefs, as mayors and city councilors, as school trustees and regional district directors. Women have been activists in various community organizations, and those with professional training have brought education, legal assistance, medical services and business skills. Women authors, journalists and historians recorded the events and customs of their times. A playwright and drama enthusiast started a vibrant theatre tradition, which continues in Williams Lake to this day. Artists reflected the beauty, variety, and historic changes in the region in their work. A few women reached out to help bridge cultural differences and to protect and promote a rich Aboriginal and multicultural heritage.

This book offers a small sampling of the women and their stories of the Cariboo Chilcotin, expanding beyond the scope of the original focus of breaking gender barriers. There were and are many other women whose stories were not submitted for this project. Hopefully, they too will be included in a future publication.

Early Days

A Melding of Cultures

Doreen Armes

BY BARB COUPÉ

*I*n an odd way, I already know this lady who I am about to interview for the first time. We have never met but I have heard snippets of her life story from a co-worker, her grandson Chris Armes. From time to time, her Cariboo adventures dominate our coffee-room chatter; Chris beams with pride in the telling of her tales.

Doreen Armes is ninety-four years of age and looks as spry and vigorous as an eighty-year-old. She is puttering in her garden when we meet, disparagingly dismissive of her cane. She informs me with a wide grin that it is for balance only—she can walk just fine, thank you!

We sit at her dining room table, and over tea and cookies she begins to reminisce. Her eyes grow reflective as she surveys the pictures of family and loved ones scattered throughout the room. On the east wall, Model T's trundle down Mackenzie Avenue in 1920s' Williams Lake. In the snapshot below, friends and neighbours picnic atop Dog Creek Mountain circa 1934, and gracing the adjacent wall, the young men of the Dog Creek hockey team smile, frozen in the sepia of the 1930s. But it is her husband Frank who catches my eye. Taken in the Dog Creek Valley, the picture shows a vigorous ninety-two-year-old rancher, looking dapper in his stockman's felt hat and blue jacket. He is posed amongst the pines in front of Brigham Lake, a lake he created back in the 1930s.

Doreen Armes in 1956 when she was principal of Skyline Elementary School in Williams Lake.

Doreen's voice continues to weave her story around me. Synchronized with the flow of her conversation, her three cuckoo clocks tick away time. I settle into my chair, tape recorder running, and pen in hand. Her story unfolds and I listen, staring into the sparkling eyes of a timeless young woman.

The day dawned warm and dusty that early September morning in 1929. At the Ashcroft Canadian National Railway station, a naïve, city-bred eighteen-year-old named Doreen Pollitt disembarked from the steam locomotive hissing on the tracks. Doreen was a newly minted teacher, an honours graduate from the Vancouver Normal School, the teachers' college of the day. She had expected to find a position in the city, but times were lean and only two teaching vacancies existed in the province—one in the Queen Charlottes and the other in the small interior community of Dog Creek. Doreen knew where and what the Charlottes were, islands surrounded by the North Pacific Ocean, but Dog Creek was a mystery. However, because she abhorred large bodies of water, Doreen had no choice: Dog Creek would be her destination and her destiny. Instead of the moist cedar-garbed slopes of coastal rainforests, she would head inland to dry hills of grass and lodge-pole pine. Her first inkling of the remoteness of the community came after a fact-finding trip to the railway office. No one there had ever heard of Dog Creek, and only after searching their maps could they tell her that the nearest station was Ashcroft. Dog Creek was a further 160 kilometres to the northwest.

Her mind made up, she applied for and was accepted into the position, much to the consternation of her mother, a dedicated urbanite who feared and dreaded the isolation and solitude of rural life. But Doreen persevered. Soon the Secretary/Treasurer of the Dog Creek School Association, A.J. Drinkell, wired instructions—she would be met in Ashcroft by one of the local ranchers, Charlie Place, and driven to her new home.

So at 5:30 in the morning, Doreen stood alone at the station, eyes bleary from the long overnight journey. As she blinked her day into existence, she became captivated by the arid sage-studded hills and the building promise of the day's heat. Something inside her clicked and despite the lack of a welcoming party, she felt the first stirrings of belonging. She resolutely strode to the one dominant building on the street, correctly assuming that this structure was the hotel. Here she would meet Mr. Place. But the hour was early and Charlie was still fast asleep. The friendly desk clerk kindly advised her to catch a few hours of rest, pointing out that she faced a long journey. Quietly, she tucked her petite frame into one of the large comfortable chairs in the lobby and promptly dozed off. What seemed like five minutes later, she awoke to the raucous squawks and calls of the hotel parrot as he whistled in appreciation at the ladies in the lobby. An hour or two had passed. After freshening up, she discovered a tall, well-built man striding into the room. He was clad in outdoor work-clothes, Doreen's first view of a rancher's "uniform." After a very welcomed breakfast, they headed off on the last leg of her journey.

Doreen soon realized her trip would be a quiet one; her new companion was a man of few words, and she herself was no chatterbox—so much the better for concentrating on the scenery. At first, she found this silent drive into the barren countryside nerve-wracking. She couldn't help contrasting the dried golden-brown grasses and scattered sagebrush with the velvet-green lushness of Vancouver shrubbery. A different world was passing by her car window. But Charlie's quiet, dependable manner inspired confidence, and she eventually relaxed. From Ashcroft they twisted and turned towards Clinton, where they connected with the main Cariboo Road. They followed this route until 59 Mile House, where they veered westwards towards Meadow Lake and the start of what seemed to be nothing but miles and miles of desolate Jack pine and rock. Her misgivings resurfaced. Then they came upon the Grandview Ranch, owned by Ray Pigeon, and began to wind alongside Dog Creek itself. Ten miles further they reached journey's end—the Dog Creek Stopping House. Here Charlie's wife, Ada, had organized a community-wide reception tea to welcome the new teacher. Doreen was pleased and relieved. In this verdant valley was a place where she knew she would be happy, a place she could call home.

The Dog Creek that Doreen had come to that September afternoon was a community in decline. It had its genesis in the 1850s' gold rush; the pack route to the goldfields traversed the valley where travellers found easy winter grazing for pack animals. A settlement soon sprang up. In the 1870s, the population swelled as the Chinese moved in to mine Fraser River gold. In his memoir, *Dog Creek: A Place in the Cariboo*, Hilary Place (son of Charlie) noted that during the 1880s his grandfather, Joseph Smith Place, arrived to a bustling town. Several hundred people supported three large stores, four hotels, a dance hall and two houses of ill repute. Cabins were scattered everywhere. As well, Dog Creek boasted the first privately built flour mill on the British Columbia mainland, constructed in 1861 by Charlie Brown. In later years, a sawmill/planer also operated in the community.

But the collapse of the gold rush, the consolidation of small ranches into larger ones, and improvements in communication and transportation all contributed to a dwindling population. By 1929, Dog Creek had reverted to a small, quiet community, many of its older buildings abandoned and deteriorating. But the original stopping house, Doreen's new home, survived. Parts of its structure predated the gold rush. Over the years, this two-storey log building grew under the ownership of the Place family, becoming a twenty-two-room hotel as well as the headquarters of the Dog Creek Ranch. At the time of Doreen's arrival, the Places had lost control of the ranch to a mining broker, James Armes, but the stopping house still served as a hotel. For thirty dollars a month, Doreen rented a room with a separate entrance and a covered porch that opened onto a lawn and lilac bushes. Board and laundry were also included. Across the street was the store, and a short walk away lay the schoolhouse.

"I thought you were paid to teach him, not smell him."

— NOTE FROM A PARENT

The school was a recent addition to Dog Creek. Constructed in 1926 from locally milled timbers, it existed largely through the efforts of Ada Place, who had generously used a personal inheritance to purchase desks and other supplies. To Doreen's young eyes, this school was like nothing she had ever seen before. She had been trained in complex, well-supplied urban facilities with vast resources and well-equipped playgrounds. The little schoolhouse at Dog Creek was a primitive one-room affair divided at the back by a cloakroom and heated by a wood stove. Water was collected from a nearby irrigation ditch, and the school was serviced by his-and-her outhouses. While textbooks and basic supplies were available, other resources were almost non-existent. There was no library; reference materials and craft supplies were very limited. In later years, Doreen was to think, "Thank goodness for radio and the Eaton's catalogue!" After taking stock of her new work place, Doreen gave herself a firm talking to. She was here to teach the students and, using whatever she could find, that was just what she was going to do!

Eleven students attended the school that year; all except one were related to Charlie and Ada Place. They ranged from grades one to nine with no students in grade five. Thus, not only did Doreen have to deal with primitive conditions and sparse supplies, she also had to cope with diverse curricula—a stressful situation for a fledgling teacher. But she soon discovered that her students were eager and keen, and that discipline was not an issue. They were a joy to teach.

For the first month, Doreen found the after-school hush to be the loneliest time as she spent the late afternoon marking and preparing for the next day. But this loneliness faded as she became more and more connected to her students and the community. Besides the regular lessons, there were concerts to organize; games to play; picnics, hikes and other outdoor adventures to experience; and a student newspaper to produce. She was particularly proud of her students' efforts on this newspaper. With the help of Mr. Drinkell, the children put together a comprehensive community paper and, in the process, broadened their horizons into the outside world. When winter settled in, Doreen was surprised to discover that no one in the community skated despite an abundance of natural outdoor rinks. Promptly she ordered herself a pair of skates and others soon followed suit. Later she would recall that the women were quite content to simply skate, but that the men insisted on making it competitive. She therefore encouraged them to play hockey. Hilary Place would later credit Doreen with being the founder of hockey in Dog Creek.

Doreen's days became full. And an extra sparkle sprang into her life—romance. During dinner on that first evening, Doreen met a good-looking young man who had been working out on the range all day. His name was Frank Armes, the owner's son, and he graciously offered to drive her around the community, to show her the sights and sounds of Dog Creek. Was this a case of love at first sight? Very likely, for a courtship soon followed, and in December of 1931 they were wed. Doreen had truly found her heart's foundation here in this tiny hamlet of ranches.

Following the custom of the times, Doreen left her teaching post for marriage. At this point, Frank was looking for work. His father had sold the Dog Creek ranch, and Charlie Place had reclaimed his family home. After a three-month stint on the coast vainly searching for employment, the young couple decided to return to Dog Creek, where at least they would be able to grow their own food. The Depression had gained momentum, and jobs were hard to find. Doreen and Frank moved into Casey House, a small building down the road from the Dog Creek Ranch. With Frank soon working for the Highways Ministry as well as for various ranches in the area, Doreen settled into a life of homemaking.

In the spring of 1936, the Armes decided to tackle gold mining. Times were still tough (beef on the hoof was selling at five cents or less a pound) and they needed cash. At this point, Bob, their first child, was four years old. Doreen could have stayed behind, but she would have none of that—she might miss an adventure or two! So they bundled up their possessions and joined Louis Krause, Frank Sakoutzki and George Thompson on the gravel bars of the Fraser River. Just getting there was excitement enough. They relayed all their equipment first by Chevy Coupe to the road's end, then by horse and democrat down a steep slope to the water's edge, and finally by a large and sturdy home-made boat driven by a powerful outboard motor. During the crossing, Doreen was dismayed to see large chunks of ice floating downriver, but they reached the gravel bar safely and set up camp.

Miles from anyone, tucked in a poplar grove on the banks of the river, a small tent-city sprang up; Doreen thought of it as their own little kingdom. Three tents were erected: one for cooking and dining, another for Doreen, Frank and Bob, and the last for the three bachelors. Conditions were rustic: rice bags served as flooring, folded blankets became mattresses and beds were constructed simply of knotted ropes hung from posts. Doreen cooked on a camp stove that boasted a stovepipe oven, a bulging section of pipe that encased an inner liner to carry away the smoke. A door opened onto a small shelf that held two loaf pans—no store-bought bread for this crew. Doreen was delighted to discover that housework was a breeze: no floors to mop, furniture to dust or windows to wash. And the weather co-operated too!

The work was steady and sleep did not have to be coaxed. Spring turned into summer and when the river rose suddenly one night, the miners found themselves fleeing to higher ground. The river surged so quickly that people in Dog Creek and Williams Lake were positive that this little band of miners had been swept away by the late spring torrents. Interesting scenery sometimes floated downstream on the high water: one day a kayaker paddled past and the next, somebody's chicken house sailed by. But despite such distractions, the group persevered—gold was their goal that summer.

The men built timbered sluice boxes called grizzlies. Water was pumped into these gravel-filled boxes and filtered through a metal screen and blanket. Doreen's job was to carefully lower the blanket into a water-filled galvanized tub and to swish the sodden mass repeatedly until the black sand was released. After the sand settled, she drained the water and poured the leavings into a gold pan. As she worked the fines, a distinct line of gold appeared. Mercury was added to coagulate the gold and then burned off in the hot coals of the cookstove. No one stayed in the tent at this stage; the poisonous fumes were allowed to dissipate as lumps of near-pure gold cooled in the ashes. Payday came when Doreen and the others trouped into Williams Lake to trade their hard-wrought gleanings for $29 an ounce at Mackenzie's General Store. Fortunes were not made, but enough cash was earned for them to carry on.

At the end of the summer, Frank received some very welcomed news—a ranch manager's job was his for the taking. Colonel Victor Spencer, the heir to Spencer's Department Store, sent a rider down into the mining camp to offer Frank employment on the Gaspard Ranch, two miles up the valley from the Dog Creek Ranch. Doreen and her family were going home. When they first moved to the Gaspard, they had few amenities. Running water was found only in the creek and made its way to the house via two galvanized buckets that sat on a bench near the kitchen door. The outhouse was a standard feature, built facing the bank of the creek a suitable distance away from the house. Light was supplied by a half-dozen kerosene lamps; shining the chimneys, trimming the wicks and filling the coal-oil bowls were daily chores. The two gas lamps, with their fragile mantles, also had to be filled and pumped up. Then modern times struck. Colonel Spencer erected a hydro-electric plant in the creek and wired all the buildings for electricity. Doreen was finally able to cook on an electric range. When the electrometer on the wall showed the electric current running too high, she would simply turn on some stove elements. They lived here on this ranch until 1949 when Victor's daughter, Barbara, became manager. During these

Doreen Armes in 2004 at the age of ninety-two.

years their family grew: Bob was joined in 1937 by Gordon, who was closely followed by Dorothy in 1938. And Allan made a surprise appearance in 1947. For this period of her life, Doreen worked as homemaker—family was her focus and her centre.

After the Gaspard Ranch, the family moved to the Nicola Stock Farms near Merritt; here too Frank was ranch manager. A few years later, they headed for Forest Grove where Frank was employed cutting railroad ties destined for Britain. Then in 1953, Doreen learned that the teacher's position in Dog Creek was vacant; she and a six-year-old Allan returned to her former school. Frank was very supportive of her decision; he knew that she enjoyed teaching as much as he did ranching. Thus at forty-two years old, she restarted her teaching career, a career that was to span the next twenty-three years. Bob was twenty-one at this point, and Gord and Dot were attending high school in Vancouver, living with their grandparents. Frank was working out of Williams Lake by then, hauling freight and selling fresh fruit and vegetables. In 1954, Doreen joined him, becoming principal of Sky-line, the new elementary school in Williams Lake.

She thrived as a teacher/principal and enjoyed having other teachers to work with. However, she found town children were not as dedicated to school as the ones at Dog Creek—there were many more distractions in the larger community. But still, she enjoyed all her students and had to deal with few discipline or playground problems. One day, the teacher of the primary grades, Mrs. O'Dell, brought a somewhat humorous situation to her attention. It seemed that a young fellow in grade one infrequently bathed or changed his clothes, and his aroma was steadily worsening. Mrs. O'Dell therefore sent a discreet note home to the boy's mother requesting that he be cleaned up. The mother complied but sent a note back saying, "I thought that you were paid to teach him, not smell him!" In later years, this anecdote was to become one of Doreen's favourite teaching tales.

The years at Skyline were busy ones, and the student population swelled. Finally, a new school was commissioned and the staff at Skyline had a say in its design, an open-air concept with study carrels—revolutionary for its time. The school was called Kwaleen, a Shuswap word for "Bark of the Birch," in honour of the birch trees growing on site. In 1966, Kwaleen opened, and Doreen became its first principal. A few years later, Doreen moved to Crescent Heights where she taught until retirement at age sixty-five. For most of her Williams Lake teaching career, Frank and Doreen lived in town, on North Lake-side. But during the last year at Crescent Heights, they had moved to the Canyon View Ranch situated along the eastern slopes of the Fraser River in the Sheep Creek Bridge area. For a short while, Frank operated a feedlot on this property. They then retired to Chimney Valley where they lived with Allan and his family for four or five years. Here Doreen found a new hobby—beekeeping, learning the art from Hugh Mahon, a long-time Cariboo beekeeper. In the mid-1980s, they followed their son Bob down to the Oka-nagan where he managed the R.J. Bennett ranch in Winfield. But they heard the Cariboo calling. In 1991, they returned to Williams Lake, to the house where Doreen lives to this day, keeping company with daughter, Dot, and son-in-law, Hank Unrau.

The strident caws of her cuckoo clocks suddenly interrupt Doreen. Her voice falls silent. I sense that she is weary. We have covered much territory in our final interview. As for me, I am still riding the waves of her memories, trying to connect with that young woman of long ago. Her daughter, Dot, has given me a token of thanks; a bookmark made from the official tartan of Williams Lake. It lies quietly in my hand, and as I run my fingers over the colours, I realize that Doreen is threaded into the history of the Cariboo much like the yarns of this fabric are woven into cloth. I fall into a trap common to how we perceive the elderly; surely Doreen must be nostalgic, even sad, for those good old days. I am firmly put to rights. With a shake of her head, she gently admonishes me. Of course she loved those days and cherishes them deeply, but they are in the past. She is not one who misses things; she looks to the future and celebrates life. As if giving me an example, she suddenly changes the topic and berates herself for missing the latest space shuttle launch. And then I understand. Here is a wise woman, one who lives fully in the present and rejoices in the gifts surrounding her. She continues to look out into the world with those eighteen-year-old eyes. The teacher is teaching, and learning still.

EDITOR'S NOTE

This account was originally written in 2005. Sadly, Doreen passed away on May 11, 2009, at the age of ninety-seven.

Veera Bonner relaxes on a log fence at Bull Canyon beside the Chilcotin River.

Veera Bonner

BY LINDA-LOU HOWARTH

Veera Bonner was born a month premature on August 25, 1918. Her father and mother, Frank and Hattie Witte, and her two older sisters, Irene and Hazel, lived on a pre-emption above the Chilcotin River they called the Chilcotin Place. This land is now the upper end of Deer Creek Ranch. The day Veera was born, her father was away putting up hay on contract for Chilco Ranch at a faraway meadow called the Wilson Meadow. This summer day after milking the cows, Hattie felt labour pains coming on. Since she was a month premature, she knew she needed to get word to her mother, Nellie Hance, who lived twenty-five kilometres away across the Chilcotin River at the TH Ranch in Hanceville.

Hattie explained to Irene, who even at three-and-a-half years old was a responsible little girl, why she had to go. She left bread and milk within reach on the table, and impressed upon Irene that she must make sure that two-year-old Hazel got food too. How heart-wrenching that must have been for Hattie to leave her little children not knowing what could happen as she left for help.

Hattie set off on foot, walking the three kilometres downriver to Dan Macauley's place. Stopping to rest when the pains came on, she reached her neighbour's place, where Margaret Macauley made Hattie comfortable and Dan Macauley set off as quickly as possible with team and buggy to get her mother.

Mrs. Hance had previously delivered babies for Mrs. Macauley, and there were phones in the valley across the river, so Nellie called Doctor Wright at Alexis Creek just in case. Dr. Wright immediately made his way to Hanceville and accompanied Nellie Hance and Dan Macauley across the river to the Macauley ranch. There they picked up Hattie, whose labour pains had become more intense, and brought her back home where her two young daughters were still waiting safe and sound after several hours. Veera was born there later that day, a month early without complications.

"A swamp meadow makes a better poor man's ranch."

— FRANK WITTE

A few years later the Wittes left the Chilcotin Place and moved further back into the bush to an isolated meadow in the Whitewater country above Vedan Ranch, fifty kilometres up a rugged road from Big Creek. "A swamp meadow makes a better poor man's ranch," Frank always said. By then a fourth child, Duane, had been born, and the family, with four small children, lived in a one-room cabin that Frank built.

One day young Duane became violently ill. It was feared he had eaten some snowberries that were toxic to his system. Fortunately Frank was home and he quickly got the horses assembled while Hattie threw together a box of food and packed a suitcase. With the three girls bundled into the back of the wagon and the sick baby in his mother's arms, they set out on the 120-kilometre journey with team and heavy iron-wheeled wagon for the hospital in Alexis Creek.

The first fifty mountainous kilometres to the Robison Ranch were the worst. There they borrowed a lighter rig and pushed the horses another forty kilometres to Hanceville where Frank put his tired team in the barn and the girls were left with their grandmother, Nellie Hance. Hattie's brother, Judd Hance, used fresh horses and a light buggy to drive Frank, Hattie and young Duane the final thirty kilometres to Alexis Creek. There Dr. Wright performed a near miracle and saved the baby's life. After weeks of anxious attention, Duane recovered, though he had to learn to walk all over again.

About a year and a half later the Wittes were camped in the Whitewater putting up hay on a swamp meadow, when Frank's father, George Witte, arrived from the States for a visit. He persuaded the family to move back home with him to Twisp, Washington, so the children could go to school. Frank could take over Geo's Butcher Shop in town there, he reasoned.

Frank and Hattie agreed that the offer sounded good, so Hattie and the children made the journey to Washington with George in his car, while Frank finished haying and made arrangements for someone to care for his stock over the winter. Then he went south by train.

A winter scene of Veera Bonner's home on Fletcher Lake near Big Creek.

All too soon both Frank and Hattie were lonesome for the Chilcotin. Though they did well financially and the two older girls had started school in Twisp, their hearts pined for Canada, especially since Frank had become a Canadian citizen four years earlier in 150 Mile House.

So after a year, they gave up the security of town life and headed back to the wilderness. This time they made the trip in a Willys Overland touring car and camped the first night on the Canadian side of the border at Osoyoos Lake. They settled in the community of Big Creek and named their ranch the Circle Lazy "A" after their cattle brand. Through Hattie's determined efforts, a school was opened and these country kids got a good education, walking two miles to and from, five days a week, winter and summer.

Frank and the other fathers built a log schoolhouse in a central location above Bambrick Creek, with a lean-to woodshed in the back. Frank made a table for the teacher's desk, benches, and a tall cupboard for books. Hattie hung curtains made from flour sacks dyed green, and the Bambricks papered the inside walls. The other family, the Blenkinsops, did their share as well, donating all the necessities for a classroom.

Veera started writing bits and pieces for the newspaper while she was still in her teens and thought she wanted to write a book. Once she asked Riske Creek author, Eric Collier, if he could give her some advice. "You don't want to write a book!" he told her. "It's a lot of damned work!"

However Veera's sister Hazel's vision and determination was to get her started. "Veera

Veera Witte (Bonner) cooks up a meal over a campfire during haying season in the Chilcotin. In the background is a chuck wagon packing a hay rake.

can do anything I set my mind to," she used to quip.

And with encouragement and help from her sisters, the book, *Chilcotin: Preserving Pioneer Memories*, by the Witte Sisters, came out in 1995, published by Heritage House. Veera did the writing for the book, but she says the project was a combined effort by all three Witte sisters.

"Irene was a big help with the upper country section," Veera says. "Both Irene and Hazel were instrumental in gathering stories from other people." The book is now in its second printing.

In June 1941 Veera married Jim Bonner and they had two children, Lynn now of Riske Creek, and Trena (Plummer) of Big Creek. Eventually the marriage ended, and in 1959 Veera took up land on Fletcher Lake near Big Creek and moved there with the kids. She started a resort business there called Bin-Goh-Sha, renting log cabins, boats and camping spaces, serving meals and boarding crews. She also worked out in Williams Lake during the winters until her business was established.

In November 1972 Fletcher Lake was frozen smooth with no snow on it and Veera was out skating when a hunter came from a cabin and put his snow machine on the ice. There was no snow on the land, and the hunter suggested he should give her a tow around the lake. Veera foolishly agreed. Coming back to shore she fell, breaking her hip. Friends from Onward Ranch, who stopped in to visit, took her in their station wagon to the hospital in Williams Lake.

Veera spent a month in the hospital and over the years has had a total of four hip operations on that leg; the last in 2003. Fortunately Veera was still able to dance. But she's not able to square dance, the one thing she really wanted to do. Another favourite activity was walking in the wind, but that was never the same. Veera never did skate again.

The Lord has helped Veera through all these years and she never worried when times were lean in the beginning. She knew He'd help her and He always did. Family and friends were always there for Veera, too.

The biggest changes she has noticed are the roads and population. When Veera moved to Fletcher Lake, there was only Willy George and Julianna Setah and their family living on Fletcher Lake. Veera could see their dim kerosene lamplight across the lake at night. Now there are many houses on Fletcher Lake. Roads were impassable in the spring when she first got there, and iffy in places any time it rained. There was only occasional snow-plowing, and sanding was unheard of. Now roads are excellent in summer and winter.

Veera began writing for the *Williams Lake Tribune* when Clive Stangoe owned the paper. She was called the "rural correspondent" back then.

Hazel's husband, Scotty Litterick, built Veera's little cabin when she first settled on Fletcher Lake. Later, her son, Lynn, helped Scotty add on to the log cabin. Then another building was made as a bunkhouse for Lynn, along with a small garage. Now Veera has four cabins that can be rented, and her own house is surrounded by a vegetable garden and lovely flowers.

As we chatted I couldn't help but admire the awesome view, the quietness, the birds and Veera's company. Along with lots of tea, buns and wonderful information, I thoroughly enjoyed myself. Veera is very interesting to chat with. My final, "Well, I better go!" took about an hour because I kept wandering around admiring everything and questioning. It was a wonderful visit.

EDITOR'S NOTE
This article appeared in *Casual Country*, 2008.

Gerry Bracewell

I was born on July 11, 1922, in Northern Alberta to a Scottish and Irish mother, and an English father, and was raised on the prairie. I had a happy outdoor childhood, picking crocuses for Mom with my three-year-old brother, catching gophers for pets, filling a small jar with fireflies, and then throwing them into Mom's bedroom, hollering "Happy birthday, Mom!" We two kids were inseparable. Our Dad died of spinal meningitis when I was five.

My mom said I was born at Half-Way Lake, Alberta—not in a hospital. Mom had a midwife who came to settlers' homesteads to deliver their babies. She must have done a good job for Mom, because she named me after the lady, in appreciation. I guess like: "This one's for you, Ethel!"

I so hated that name all through my school years, and it wasn't as though I had a choice. I wasn't given a middle name like most kids. So I had a nickname. My friends called me "Frisky" because I was into everything athletic: horseback riding like the wind, bareback (no saddle allowed until I was sixteen), and I played sports too, especially softball. I was captain of the school's girl team, and was sent to a city sports day to represent my country school. I won a few ribbons that day. The older kids in grades eight and nine would put on Saturday night dances at our school. We would hold polka competitions.

My partner and I won out over everyone else. The floor was tilting badly, and the room was spinning violently before the music stopped. And we had won. I was fourteen.

We lived on a farm, raising a few cattle, wheat and a big garden. We always had milk, meat, and vegetables, so we kids knew nothing about the Depression. I walked three miles to a country school. At seven, I broke a calf to ride. Then, later, Mom bought a horse for us to ride to school. Every weekend, my brother Bob and I were in the bush building tipis, playing Indians, and catching rabbits or ducks. In grade nine I had to walk five miles to school. I soon developed a good memory for my lessons, and passed into grade ten in midterm, and then into grade eleven in June. After graduating, I found a summer job herding range cattle to keep them out of the bordering grain fields with wire fences. The forty dollars I earned financed my November migration to Vancouver, BC, accompanied by my older sister.

> *"My heart belonged to the open range."*
>
> — GERRY BRACEWELL

When I attended my first Christmas concert near Tofield, Alberta, I wasn't in school yet. Probably four-and-a-half years old. The Christmas tree was a poplar tree with creeping cedar branches or runners tied along its boughs. Every one of the children received a present off that tree except me. I was too little to realize that oversight. But on Monday, when the teacher and students dismantled the tree, they found a beautiful string of blue-green beads twined among the cedar boughs with my name on it. That colour, teal blue, has been a favourite of mine ever since.

I was seventeen-and-a-half when I travelled to BC in search of mountains. Instead I became the full-time governess for an adorable toddler whose parents both worked. Living in posh Shaughnessy Heights in Vancouver among blooming apple trees in March was quite a change, but my heart belonged to open range, livestock, and pioneering. By May I abandoned Vancouver for a job on a Chilcotin ranch cooking, cleaning, milking, and playing with two small children. I had been hired on the ranch as a general cook, but I could ride and herd cattle on weekends. What a privilege.

Then I moved deeper into the Chilcotin where soaring 10,000-foot peaks surrounded Tatlayoko Lake. I knew I was home. There were horses to train, cowboying, gardening, milking, cooking, and in season, hunting with guide outfitter Mr. Kennon Beverly (K.B.) Moore.

K.B. Moore trained me up through the ranks as a "C" guide for three years, a "B" guide for two years, then I became an "A" guide, the class of guide outfitter I am today. Then K.B. retired. "You can do it now," he said.

Gerry Bracewell is bundled into a horse-drawn sleigh for a perilous thirty-seven kilometre, mid-winter journey from Tatlayoko Lake to the Graham Ranch in Tatla Lake to give birth to her first son, Marty Moore.

Two years after I arrived in Tatlayoko I married K.B.'s only son, Beverly Kennon Moore, who was being drafted into the army. It seemed like the right thing to do at the time. When my husband's contingent was shipping out, he developed measles, and remained in Canada, and was able to come home on furlough occasionally.

My first birthing experience turned out to be impossible. It was January, so the stage had quit running. There were no snow ploughs. We had only our team and sleigh to get me twenty-three miles out to Tatla Lake where I was to meet with a doctor. A neighbour had ridden on horseback those thirty-seven kilometres to the only phone, a party line, relayed halfway to Williams Lake by Alexis Creek, to get a doctor for me. The doctor had to come with Bill Sharp, the village police officer in Williams Lake, by car, often shovelling through drifts along the 230 kilometres of Chilcotin Road.

When one of our team became exhausted from pulling the sleigh through eighteen inches of snow, Mr. Moore (the grandpa-to-be) borrowed a neighbour's horse. Our other horse, a mean-spirited ex-rodeo bronc named Blackoby, after Mr. Moore's banker, soldiered on. He won much praise from all of us. We arrived at sundown in Tatla Lake ahead of the doctor.

The hospitable Graham family put me into the master bedroom off the kitchen. I lapsed into sleep several times, finally aroused by much hustle and bustle when the doctor arrived. He was washing his hands at the bedroom sink. They had forgotten the rubber gloves. A washcloth was draped over my face and ether poured onto it. I zonked out.

A wild dream, all in technicolour, took over. It was about a long, colourful queue of people winding down a grassy hillside to a free-standing door in the valley. They were going through and disappearing. When I finally reached the door, just as my foot raised and I was about to step through, someone standing by my side said, "I want that one," and pulled me out to stand beside him. Then, zip! I was back on the hilltop to wind my way down with the others to the door again, where all went through but then disappeared from sight.

Again, I attempted to step through, but was again physically pulled out of position with the words, "I want that one." I then stood alongside what seemed to be a tall man. Then the dream changed. Then I heard a baby cry.

I was awakened to see a light bulb spinning crazily overhead. As it slowed and steadied, I saw Dr. Mackenzie splinting my baby's leg. My son was delivered alive after our seventy-four hours of hopeless labour. His right femur had to be broken mid-thigh to deliver him feet-first. It was a partial breach.

Hodgson's stage wasn't due to come through for two weeks. Within two days I developed a devastating fever with chills, which I fought with every fibre of my being. These were the days before antibiotics. I couldn't die now, I had a baby to care for. Every day my baby's splints worked down and had to be reset by the wonderful Graham family. Hodg-

Gerry Bracewell sits with her son Marty beside a campfire on a beef drive to Williams Lake.

Gerry Bracewell with her two oldest sons, Marty, standing, and infant Barry in Gerry's arms.

son's stage finally arrived and took me into the Williams Lake Hospital. My baby was admitted, but not me.

Dr. Pump was the only resident doctor, but he was a good one. He re-broke my baby's leg, taped small square blocks onto the soles of his feet and screwed cup hooks into the blocks. Long strings were fastened to the hooks, with the other ends holding weights dangling off the end of the crib. The baby lay on his back with both feet up at a right angle to his body. In a month I would be allowed to take him home.

Hodgson's stage returned us to Tatla Lake, where our team, sleigh, and a driver awaited us. It was a long, cold thirty-seven kilometres mostly in the dark on February 24, 1944. Within a mile of the ranch, we had to abandon the sleigh and my box of apples because the road was too icy for the horses. The teamster took them up onto brushy hillsides to find safe footing. I carried my baby in the freezing dark over that icy road, praying that we would not fall. The lamp in the window was a halo of gold. Grandpa Moore was waiting up for us. He lovingly accepted his grandson from my weary arms.

The war soon ended. My husband returned to ranching and a baby brother for Marty was born in June. But this idyllic family life was not to be. Interference separated us. My husband left to aid his mother with her ranch, and she found him another soul mate. Eventually he filed for divorce.

Since there were no babysitters then, my sons went everywhere with me. I was the cowboy for the outfit. Grandpa Moore ran the ranch, taking the boys with him to do the irrigating. The boys loved that, splashing through the sun-warmed ditches and pools. I also washed clothes by hand, baked bread and other goods, cooked meals, milked the cows and raised a garden.

Grandpa was a Class A guide, which permitted him to take hunting clients after whatever big game was in season. Whenever I could find a neighbour lady to watch over my boys for the day, I'd go along to learn the business. The road ended at our ranch and game animals were numerous, so we could hunt out of the ranch and return in the evening.

Grandpa had apprenticed as a guide outfitter with Ralph Edwards of Lonesome Lake. With spring bear hunting and fall moose, mule deer, and bear hunting, he needed

Everlasting Love

The stalwart young Cowboy rode into the West;
Throughout the Chilcotin his steed was the best.
He rode through the grasslands, to the mountains so grand
Met a young Indian maiden, and asked for her hand...
But She was a Princess; her Father the Chief!
Aghast was her family in their disbelief
That this handsome young Cowboy should be so naïve
As to ask for this maiden, his heart on his sleeve.
The greying old Chieftain...the last of his breed...
Scorned anyone White; so to mix with His seed
Was unheard of; unwelcome; and reason to fight!
So, while the drums sounded, they stole off in the night.
They rode through the dark just as far as they could,
Then, at last, made their camp in a sheltering wood.
Deep into the Mountains, where no man had roamed
They rode, till they found the right site for their home.
The Cowboy got busy; a log cabin soon stood
Near a creek, in a clearing surrounded by woods.
Moose and deer, wolves and coyotes, and even the bear,
Used to crossing the clearing, would stop now and stare...
So meat for their larder was always at hand.
This practical couple could live off the land:
Dried berries; fish; roots—she served a good stew,
Cozied in their log cabin when Winter winds blew.
The dried skins of beaver, of muskrat, and mink
Piled high in a corner, gave one pause to think
How this happy young couple were hatching a plan
To re-visit the Outside for word of her clan.
Come Spring-time they bundled the hides on a horse
And set out for Chilcotin, to fur-trade, of course,
The Hudson's Bay Company then traded in skins;
Which made for a meeting with other Indians.
By Moccasin Grapevine word reached them one day;
The old Chief (her Father) was wasting away.
"I must go to see him, before he departs,"
She pleaded. Her husband agreed from the start.
And so they—together—returned to her kin;
The family, rejoicing, all welcomed them in.
The old Chief, now feeble, accepted the Man
Who made off with his daughter, but honoured her hand.
He had proved her protector, the old Chief acquiesced,
And sounded the drums to announce a great Feast.
Re-united with Family, they now could abide,
And join ever after at the Home fireside.

EDITOR'S NOTE
This poem by Gerry Brace-well is about a romantic love story tryst that is well-known in Chilcotin lore. It involved American George Powers and his Tsilhqot'in "Indian Prin-cess" wife Jessie, who eloped to the far reaches of the Chilco-tin Plateau, to Tatlayoko Val-ley then Charlotte Lake so they could live together in peace.

Powers came from Washing-ton state in 1914, reportedly connected to the notorious outlaw Plummer Gang. How-ever he never displayed wan-ton, anti-social behaviour, and had the reputation of being a quiet, well-dressed cowboy. George and Jessie lived their lives faithfully together, and spent their last days in an old log house near Hanceville.

an assistant guide. Because I loved the wilderness and the adventure of stalking game animals, Grandpa Moore took me along to learn the ropes. I could only go when I had someone responsible to stay with my little boys, and that was difficult to find.

One day Grandpa Moore asked, "So how about it? I want to quit." This began my fifty years as an A-Guide outfitting and guiding hunters for moose, mountain goats, mule deer, and black and grizzly bears that preyed on our cattle. Advertising consisted of writing thousands of letters. There were no phones back then. I always allowed two days between hunts to bake enough bread, cookies, etc., to take on my ten-day hunts as well as to supply Grandpa and the boys. We also raised a good garden and butchered our own beef. Staple items were trucked in by Hodgson stage every fortnight.

I accepted the role of guide outfitter and continued the membership with the Chilcotin Guides Association. As a guide outfitter I was responsible for advertising. Thinking I was on the right track, I put an expensive ad into *Outdoor Life* magazine, and received a dozen letters from US hunters. The letters I typed and mailed listed animals available, dates, rates, maps, and a list of suggested clothing. I also stated that I was a woman guide outfitter. Bad idea. Not one answered. From then on, letters to Gerry Bracewell were addressed to me, "Dear Sir."

On arrival, my guests accepted the fact that their guide outfitter was a woman. If there were only two in the party, I could guide them by myself. If three or four came, the ideal

number, I hired a local native or, as my sons grew older, they guided for me. All four of them are mountain men, and two are now guide outfitters. Grandpa said I should become a licenced guide because I could always see the game, so he bought an assistant's licence for me. It wasn't hard for me to learn to track, pack a horse, and to clean and skin an animal. We'd take the boys too whenever we could. They became good riders. After five years of me learning the business, Grandpa said, "You can take over. I'm retiring."

Game guide Gerry Bracewell demonstrates the art of throwing a diamond hitch on her packhorse to her hunting clients. Gerry was the first female guide outfitter in the Cariboo Chilcotin, and possibly the first in British Columbia.

He was happiest playing and working with his grandsons when they came along, so he could teach them about ranching. It was a good decision. We didn't know at that time that Grandpa's health was failing. He needed to slow down. As for me, I was right at home in the wilderness. I

Gerry Bracewell looks for game in the mountains of Tatlayoko Valley where she has made her home since 1940.

loved everything about it. I could make a comfortable camp in any unfamiliar setting, loved my horses, and trusted them to alert me to anything moving in the bush. I kept a fire going all night, and my dog and rifle were always beside me.

Female guide outfitters were not common. I was the only one in the Chilcotin, and probably in the province at that time in 1950. However, after a successful ten-day hunt in untracked wilderness with great camp food and a safe delivery for the hunters and their trophies back to their vehicles, they not only returned themselves the next year, but brought friends along, too.

It took me a while to discover that the customer is not always right. Trying to appease the odd bull-headed hunter was difficult. If I did it his way and it turned out wrong, it was my fault. So I eventually told them at the start how it was going to go, even once to the point of inviting them to leave. Especially in the case of two Mexican grizzly hunters. I had written letters to them three months prior to our May grizzly hunt listing all the details. They arrived at the ranch the evening before. We had a good meal, and they liked their cozy log cabin with a fire and warm beds. After breakfast we rode up the mountainside to a meadow where grizzlies hung out. We tied up our horses and began our stalk. I found a ten-inch fresh grizzly track. It was a sure thing. Then I asked if they had brought their hunting tags along. "Oh no, we didn't buy them. We thought we'd get the bears first," they said. Well that's where the hunt ended, right there. I took them back to the ranch and they went home. They hadn't paid in advance, either.

Some hunters expected the guide to have the deer or moose hanging up when they arrived. I had to re-educate them as to hunting ethics. But for every difficult client, there were ten who genuinely appreciated the opportunity of experiencing the wilderness setting.

It was a busy life, but chock-full of exciting adventures. By 1950 I was a fully capable rancher, building range cabins, roping, branding, and castrating our calves alone in the range corral. I broke my own horses to pack, then to ride, and trucked stock to market. Once, I roped and salvaged a range calf that I'd found near its dead mother twenty kilometres from the ranch one December 24.

When Lignum Mill moved on in the 1970s, I helped get a better school for Tatlayoko community. I was instrumental, as postmistress for Tatlayoko back in the early 1940s, to assist in preventing the closure of our post office by the federal government.

In 1953, Grandpa developed terminal cancer. He managed to visit his family in New Mexico before being hospitalized. We had a capable crew haying our big meadow when word filtered through regarding the road through the coast range about to be completed to Bella Coola. This was history in the making. It seemed to me that someone should be recording it. Grandpa had bought me a wind-up 8mm movie camera. I could do this.

In early September, after checking with my hay crew, the boys and I grabbed our sleeping bags and a little food and drove our pickup to Trails-End Lodge near Anahim Lake. There we rented two horses at sundown and were guided through the Jack pine jungles and swamps by a local native, to the Cat tracks marking the beginning of the Freedom Road made the summer before by Alf Bracewell on the Graham's D-6 Caterpillar bulldozer. At dusk we camped under a spruce tree, horses staked on the meadow on each side, rifle handy. We were saddled up and gone by daylight, following the Cat track into the distant Coast Range Mountains.

After fifty or so kilometres we arrived at Alf Bracewell's camp in time for supper. We slept soundly that night rolled up in a big tarp on the rock shelf of the gravel road. The Cats were still two weeks from meeting. Here was an excellent opportunity for recording the actual blasting and chiselling of this long-awaited roadway through the

Guide outfitter Gerry Bracewell discusses hunting strategies with a couple of hunters in the mountains of Tatlayoko Valley.

Gerry Bracewell, on horseback in front of her twenty-four room Wilderness Lodge in Tatlayoko Valley, is ready to head out on a pack trip into the Potato Mountains with some young trailriders.

mountain barrier to the little coastal village of Bella Coola.

I husbanded my precious 200 feet of 8mm film to record the highlights of this grandiose achievement, reserving enough footage for the "meeting of the Cats" in two weeks' time. The boys and I ran the "goat trail" on the steep mountainside to visit the Bella Coola crew, drilling and blasting their way toward the meeting place of the bulldozers. Because we had to return to our haying crew before the meeting of the Cats would occur, I left my camera with a competent photographer to record the historic occasion. We spent one more night dozing in our sleeping bags under the big tarp, then it was time to leave. We retraced our steps, happy in the knowledge of having achieved our goal. Some of the heroic exploits of the two road-building crews had now been recorded in action for future generations.

In September 1953, Grandpa Moore had been given only two months to live. His positive and often humourous attitude extended that time to six months. He passed away peacefully in March 1954.

Grandpa had really admired Alf Bracewell. Along about November 1953, after Alf had returned the Cat to the Graham Ranch at Tatla Lake, Grandpa sent a message to Alf to come see him. Worried about me having to run the ranch alone, Grandpa asked Alf if he was interested in "buying in" to become my business partner. Alf sold a couple of quarter sections he owned and put the proceeds toward paying off the mortgage. Grandpa

Moore engineered the legality of the partnership. Grandpa's assessment of Alf's qualities made a big impression on me. His knowledge, ability, and common sense, along with his quiet humour, won my little sons over, and eventually me. We were married in January of 1954, with Grandpa's blessing.

The ranch blossomed, new fences appeared, a Cat was purchased, my seven consecutive cattle beef drives to Williams Lake ended with Alf now hauling the cattle in his Kenworth truck. We even guided our hunting clients together that autumn of 1954 before Alf, the Cat skinner, became too immersed in clearing land, logging timber and running a sawmill to help me guide. The guide outfitting business improved with quicker mail service and a radio telephone. By now my two older sons were old enough to become my assistant guides. We had some great adventures together. Alf and I were blessed with two more boys born three years apart, who grew up to become licenced guide outfitters. My guiding and outfitting business covered a span of fifty-five years.

When the older boys left to manage their own lives, Alf and I decided to sell the ranch. Logging had siphoned off all the itinerant labour. Our health was suffering from overwork. We kept the guiding business and with the help of the two younger sons, built a twenty-four-room log lodge in the heart of our Wilderness Guiding Territory.

Susie (1958): A Short Story

The Chilcotin used to be noted for being home to herds of wild horses, mostly domesticated horses that ran wild, ranging in the hills during the summer, and rustling (pawing through snow for the long meadow-grass) on swamp meadows during the winter. The offspring from these escapees grew up wild and unbroken. Since they were also unbranded, they were free for the taking.

The young buckaroos of the Chilcotin, natives and settlers alike, considered wild horse chasing to be quite a sport. It was important, of course, to own a fast horse and to be a good rider. They could keep or sell what they caught. So on a spring day in March, cowboy Ben Wilson from a neighbouring ranch rode into our Circle X ranch yard leading a couple of two-year-old fillies, one bay, one gray—wild stock that Ben had caught out in the Wild Horse Hills. They were a present from Ben to my two little sons, Marty, three years old, and Barry, one-and-a-half years old (they are grown mountain men now). We branded the two fillies and proceeded to gentle them with lots of handling and good clover hay. We named them Susie and Millie. They grew up to be a good size, especially Susie, who showed a bit of draft horse in all the right places. When she was fully grown, she and her teammate, Lightning, powered the horse-drawn hay-mower, and the sweep, a device that was used throughout the Chilcotin to bring the windrowed hay to the slide stacker. This team worked all the horse-powered ranch jobs. It was Pete Baptiste, an excellent horseman, who first broke Susie to harness; she pulled her weight as half the team, cutting hay on a very hummocky meadow. This kind of work gentles any horse, and quickly.

After this education, Susie moved up to being trained as a pack horse. As soon as she mastered carrying weight and allowed extra "knee" space when moving through timber, she graduated to saddle horse status. We often took her on a hunting trip into the mountains, which provides further training of horses.

Susie became so dependable and responsible that we could trust her with a whole bunch of little kids lined up on her back. When Susie was only three years old, and big enough, I began breaking her to be a saddle horse by cowboying our ranch cattle, moving them south along the mountainside onto fresh grass every week. The cattle were by now about twenty-five kilometres down-range, which necessitated a camp-out, so I went prepared this day with my sleeping bag tied behind the cantle and sandwiches for myself and my dog. There was plenty of grass for Susie.

I had checked the range for stragglers for twenty kilometres. Evening was coming on, so I chose a good spot for our camp-out. There was plenty of wood. Dry limbs, broken from the big Douglas firs by heavy snows, littered the ground. Grass grew lush and green in the openings, and a creek chortled nearby. I pulled my rigging from Susie, let her roll, then staked her in a clearing and built up a fire. Then Yugo, my dog, and I shared our supper before I stockpiled a bunch of wood to keep the fire going all night (insurance against bears). At dark, I crawled into the bag with my 30.30 rifle and the firewood close by, and counted stars until I fell asleep.

Next morning I restaked Susie on fresh pasture, fed Yugo and myself, and drowned the fire with creek water. We would still be moving down-range, so my sleeping bag could be picked up on my return. I rolled it and tied it to the top of a limber poplar, which, when released, sprang upright, out of the reach of bears. Then I brought Susie in, saddled her, and we were on our way. My green-broke filly moved off willingly up the brushy mountain slope to search for cattle.

Two hours later, having ridden a mile up the mountainside and checked the alder swamp on the north side of Fossil Creek snugged in close against the rock cliffs of Potato Mountain, we had both earned a rest. We hadn't found any cattle.

The July day was idyllic. An intense blue sky with a few puffy white clouds floated north, propelled by a cool breeze off the glaciers, two bald eagles were soaring in lazy circles just below the clouds, and the air was redolent with the scent of fir needles that lay matted on the ground and baking in the sun. I sat on my chunky bay mare and gazed all about in respectful admiration. Towering above me were the escalating ramparts of Potato Mountain's 7,000-foot western rim. All about me were big fir trees, 300 to 500 years old; their ancient spreading shade had created a park-like clearing, allowing 400 metres of visibility.

I looked to the south. This fir-timbered bench seemed to continue to where Fossil Creek canyon should be, another 500 metres or so. I hoped to find a deer crossing, if possible, which would save my horse a lot of hard climbing in the future. If this proved impossible, we would have to return to the only crossing, two kilometres back downhill, cross the creek canyon, then climb back up again to check the lush range on the continuous bench on the south side of Fossil Creek.

Perhaps the sheer rock gorge coming off Potato Mountain that contained wild Fossil Creek would continue without a hospitable break to its rock walls. In that event, it would take time to scout out a game-trail crossing the creek canyon. But the day was still young and I was determined to do this.

My viewscape now swept to the right of centre. Three hundred metres off a bear was nosing the ground—a really big blonde bear. It had to be a grizzly, the first grizzly I had ever seen.

Mentally, I knew I should quietly backtrack and forget about the creek crossing for now. Curiosity caused me to ignore this inner voice—for the moment. After all, the bear was 300 metres off, and upwind from me, so therefore unaware of my presence. Bears are also notorious for having poor vision. These were my several reasons for watching just a little longer. But I hadn't reckoned on my young cowdog picking up the bear's scent and trotting off in that direction to investigate.

As I whistled a "come here" note, and the dog turned and started back, the bear's head came up. Seeing the golden flash of the collie running through the green pine-grass, it immediately came in pursuit. Two more bears of equal size and colour now appeared from behind the soapallalie bushes.

It was too late now to retreat. Those bears could easily outrun my bumble-footed filly. I decided to move into the wind, toward the canyon. Surely when they got my scent they would recognize danger and run off. I moved my horse out at a quick walk. The other two bears ignored the direction of the first, who was after my returning dog, but chose to cut across and head me off!

I sped up to a lope, my dog close behind. Now all three bears had come together and were loping 30 metres behind us. When they were directly in line with my scent, all three grizzlies stood up out of their rolling gait to sniff the breeze, their huge claws hung across their furry bellies. "Get back there you sons-o-guns," I yelled, "or I'll shoot you." Fat chance. My 30.30 held only five shells and was crammed into a stiff cowhide scabbard. That rifle would have to be my last resort if they didn't spook now. They didn't. They dropped down and kept coming.

I kicked my mare into overdrive and headed straight for the canyon's rim, praying that it would not be sheer rock. A movement from under a scraggly fir growing right on the rim caught my eye. I had surprised a dappled fawn bedded there among the shadows and sunbeams. It stood up and froze motionless.

"Watch out, baby," my mind emphatically projected as I lunged my horse toward the canyon's rim. One glance proved it to be sandy clay. I held her head up, sitting well back on her hips as we plunged over, forcing her to slide down the forty-five-degree slope on her haunches, her forelegs well out in front, sliding and feeling for footing. A dozen metres down we bottomed out and were faced then with a barrier of poplars and alders hanging out from the bank at all angles, having been undercut by high water.

Hardly slackening our pace, we launched into this tangle. The lower ones she jumped, the higher ones, some just skimming the saddle horn, we went under with me crouching low on her side, Indian-style. We reached the creek, crashed through and lunged out the other side, never looking back. That rim was lower and easy. We gained the top in three jumps and lit out through the open fir timber at full speed.

A couple of minutes later, hearing nothing from behind, I stole a quick glance back through the open park-like timber. No bears in sight. I eased my heaving mare to a slower pace and then to a walk. We were well out of the range of any bear's initial charge by now.

Dismounting, I slackened the cinch, then hugged Susie and stroked her wet neck, and complimented her on her endurance. Then, taking my 30.30 in hand, we went off walking, to cool her out. We still had cattle to check further down-range, and we had to get back home before dark.

Susie lived a long and eventful life. Her only foal was a flashy red-and-white pinto filly we named Pretty Baby, who grew up to be as reliable and stoical as Susie. Pretty Baby, in turn, gifted us with several foals, the one most like Susie is Chocolate Chip, a liver chestnut mare who regularly drops a pinto foal, all of which can be depended upon to carry our Alpine/Wilderness Adventure guests safely through the mountains.

Considering that Susie enabled me to escape the grizzlies, she more than earned her place in this Horse Memorial Park.

—by Gerry Bracewell

Emily Lulua Ekks

BY SAGE BIRCHWATER

*I*t's been a year now since Emily Ekks passed away on the shore of Kwitzeen (Cochin) Lake in the West Chilcotin. She was eighty-six years old and was bathing in the lake getting ready to go to a funeral in Anahim Lake, when she died suddenly.

In keeping with the traditions she so steadfastly upheld, Emily's headstone was set in place on June 14, 2001, a year after her death, at the family graveyard at Big Eagle (Choelquoit) Lake where she was buried.

It goes without saying that Emily, or Inkel, as her family called her, was one of a kind. In her remote corner of the Chilcotin she quietly practised the traditions of her culture: tanning hides, netting fish, drying meat and fish, sewing buckskin, making spruce root baskets, and attending various events and gatherings. She was well respected and loved by all members of the community, both native and white. As a distinguished Tsilhqot'in elder she was often called upon for advice and consulted as a historian. Wise as her days were long, it could be said that Emily's life reflected the old axiom: "The meek shall inherit the earth."

Emily lived as she always had, embracing the richness of the land. Clad in moccasins she sewed from deer skins she had tanned herself, and adorned in the rich garb of colourful cotton print, Emily caught the eye of all who met her. But it was more her demeanour

Emily Lulua Ekks' log cabin at Kwitzeen (Cochin) Lake has stood empty since Emily passed away in 2000. PHOTO SAGE BIRCHWATER

that commanded people's attention. Alert, poised, ageless. Adjectives don't really do her justice.

Indirectly I heard of Emily years before I met her. Her son Donald Lulua lived in Williams Lake when I worked for the Cariboo Friendship Society in the mid-1970s. He was a few years older than me, and had the heart to do good things for his people. Often we attended the same meetings. Though he took refuge in the comforts of street life, Donald once in a while excused himself from these trappings, saying he had to go out west to check on his mother. Then he'd be gone for a few weeks or a month or more before returning to street life again. I always wondered at this.

A few years later I met Donald at a funeral at Nimpo Lake. By then I had moved west and was living on my trapline in the mountains south of Tatla Lake, when Donald befriended me, renewing our ties. He explained the ways of a Tsilhqot'in wake to me, the several days of feasting and potlatching, and how people would come from hundreds of kilometres around to pay their respects to the departed and show support for the family. It was an important Tsilhqot'in custom, and a far cry from the death-at-an-arm's-length stoicism I had grown up with in Victoria.

Whether it was here or some place later that I met Donald's mother, I'm not sure, but it was an eye-opener to meet Donald on his own turf. It made me feel good to have a friend welcome me to ways completely foreign to my upbringing.

Emily and her husband, Donald Ekks, also lived at Tatla Lake, so it was only a matter of time before our paths crossed. Their life there can best be described as a territorial occupation rather than being tied to a single address or plot of ground, like most of the rest of us. They moved fluidly between a couple of cabins and several camping spots over an eighty-kilometre radius throughout the year, depending on the season. These were places where Emily and members of her family had stayed, year after year, generation after generation, as far back as anyone could remember.

And it seems governments of all descriptions left Emily alone. Perhaps it was the fact that she lived simply without the amenities of modern times, like running water, electricity, indoor plumbing and the like. Or maybe it was the integrity of her lifestyle, living close to the roots of her culture, that kept the paper-clutching minions of bureaucracy at bay. At any rate none of these homesites or camping spots was ever designated "Indian Reserve" by the Feds or deeded provincial fee simple lands either.

Emily Lulua Ekks sets her net at night in Kwitzeen (Cochin) Lake in 1989. For many generations her family camped at Kwitzeen Lake, even in the winter, where they set their nets under the ice and caught suckers. PHOTO SAGE BIRCHWATER

A big part of Emily's life was her ability to get around. Though she and Donald Ekks lived by themselves away from other people, they never owned a vehicle. For a while their youngest son David had a pickup truck, and they shared a cabin with him part of the year. But most of the time if Donald or Emily wanted to go somewhere, they simply stood on the side of the road until someone came by and picked them up. That's probably how I got to know them best.

It seems everyone in Tatla Lake got called upon to give Emily and Donald a ride at one time or another. In a way it was a privilege to help them out. A lift home or a longer trip to Anahim Lake, Redstone or Nemiah Valley, if you happened to be going that way. A crowded pickup cab was not an issue. Things got shuffled, stuff put in the back, or even people were loaded into the pickup truck box sometimes.

Perhaps my fondest memories are driving over the bumpy, rutted road into their cabin at Kwitzeen Lake at a snail's pace. A rabbit suddenly darts across the road and into the bush on the other side, and Emily excitedly pulls on Donald's arm. "Gugh!" she says. "Rabbit," Donald translates quietly. And other times when there was nothing to say, Emily often hummed silently to herself, almost like a mantra.

There are other moments I remember. A lazy afternoon in the hot sun at Kwitzeen Lake, old people sitting around in the high grass, fish drying on a rack above a smoky fire, and Donald introduces me to his sister Minnie, some twenty years his senior. She wants a ride into Tatla Lake, he tells me, so we all bundle into my old red truck, some sitting in the cab, others comfortably perched on the flat deck behind. As we trundle over the gravel and through the dust, I have a hard time imagining my own eighty-year-old grandmother so agile and at ease riding between swaying stock racks.

On one occasion in Tatla Lake, my friends Ted and Cyndy Abbott met up with Emily in the Graham Inn parking lot shortly after getting home from the Bella Coola maternity ward. The sparkle in Emily's eye and her excitement as she pulled back the blanket covering the newborn's face showed she had no colour or racial barriers when it came to rejoicing over a new birth.

Finally back in 1994, Emily's family decided it was time to celebrate her birthday. She was turning eighty that year, so they pulled out all stops. A band shell was constructed in the meadow next to their cabin at Kwitzeen Lake, musicians were lined up, and invitations were sent out.

I happened to be in Anahim Lake the morning of the scheduled party attending a funeral, and who should I meet there but Donald and Emily. "Aren't you supposed to be in Tatla Lake?" I queried. "Yes. Maybe we catch a ride with you?" Donald replied. You can be sure party organizers were glad to see us as we rolled in that afternoon.

"We didn't know whether they were even going to be here," a family member told me later. "We just took a chance and organized it anyway." And it worked out fine. Just like most things in Emily's eventful life.

Things haven't quite been the same around Tatla Lake since Emily passed away on June 30, 2000, in the high grass beside the lake. Donald still catches rides to Kwitzeen Lake, but stays in Ubill Lulua's larger cabin further down the lake. The little cabin he shared with Emily, built by their son David when he was fourteen years old, stands empty most days. The activities of tanning hides, netting fish and drying meat that Emily was always engaged in, have ceased now.

"We didn't know whether they were even going to be here."

— EMILY'S FAMILY

Like many other renowned Chilcotin legends, Emily "died with her boots on" as the expression goes. In her case it was moccasins. And I'm sure from her perspective, her passing was more like a momentary pause in her busy life before continuing on to the next phase of her journey. For those of us left behind it was the passing of an era. While she was here she touched us all.

God be with you, Inkel. And thanks.

EDITOR'S NOTE

This tribute to Emily Lulua Ekks was originally published by the *Williams Lake Tribune* in 2001. The story won an award at the annual Ma Murray BC Yukon Community Newspaper Awards Gala in 2002.

Marie Fletcher

HOW I BECAME A CATTLE RANCHER

Marie Fletcher married her husband Orville on May 6, 1936, shortly after she turned fifteen years old. Orville was eleven years older at twenty-six years old. They fell in love three years earlier when Marie was twelve and Orville was twenty-three. He said he met his wife Marie when she was still a school girl and decided to wait until she grew up. In the fall of 1937, the young couple with their infant daughter, Iris, bought the small ranch for $600 in the 150 Mile House area, where Orville had grown up as a foster child. They paid $100 and a horse for a down payment. Marie says the place had not been lived in for several years and resembled a disaster area.

The house that we moved into at the 150 Mile House ranch was a dream house; a nightmarish dream. But it was what came with the ranch, and what was important was the ranch.

Winter was fast approaching and our newly acquired hundred and some young cattle, via a share-for-care arrangement, needed a home, so of course the house was of little importance. Fortunately the roof didn't leak!

It was an aged log structure, built by the first pre-emptor of the land. The inside logs had just been chinked with whatever was available, and thickly covered with a mud mixture, which no doubt originally stopped every draft of cold winter air that could possibly have penetrated the log walls. But it was now crumbling away, leaving the house messy and drafty as well.

To add to these aggravations, the building had been empty for several years except for thriving families of pack rats who left their own distinctive, long-lasting scent in the big piles of trash in the corners that were their homes.

We needed a place to winter near the hay we had put up for the cattle that summer. There was no other such place, so we bought it, our first ranch.

Well, I covered the draughty places with more mud and got some rolls of heavy gray building paper and glued it onto the mud walls with a flour and flaked glue paste, and hoped it would stay put. It did.

In the meantime, our six-month-old daughter was confined to her crib in the cleanest corner available. The pack rat smell was fading. The floor however was completely unacceptable for a baby to crawl on, so I went squirrel hunting. The pelts were worth a dollar apiece. Before long, I had linoleum on the floor and Iris had a clean place to crawl.

So it went, that bit by bit, the house became liveable and home.

"The old roadhouse...had become a home."

— MARIE FLETCHER

THE 144 MILE RANCH

The 144 Mile Ranch went up for sale in the late 1940s. It was dry, rocky hillsides. "Why would you buy that pile of rocks?" was the general comment when we did just that. We had spent the first fourteen years of our marriage ranching in the higher altitudes of the Cariboo country of British Columbia.

Orville had spent most of his life battling the hardships of ranching in one of the most difficult parts of the country. This high country produced poor swamp hay, spring came late, and a short summer was followed by a long, cold winter. Rangeland consisted of endless acres of Jack pine forests with an occasional little swampy meadow.

If managed carefully one could raise cattle there, but Orville's keen blue eyes observed the difference in the livestock in the main river valleys and decided that was the place to ranch.

When the 144 Mile Ranch in the San Jose River Valley went up for sale, he saw it as an opportunity to get out of the high country and build a ranch in the valley. Never mind that it was a pile of rocks. There were sunny, dry, bunchgrass sidehills, a boon to calving cows, when in the higher country, mud, slush and snow prevailed.

There the first green grass sprouted and the deer gathered for the early spring feast. There the cows fed on the sparse but nutritious bunchgrass later into winter than they did anywhere else. There was a place to view the valley spread out below you, to watch the glorious sunsets fade and the sunrise touch the treetops with gold. These low-lying hills were called the spring fields.

The 144 Mile Ranch headquarters was only twenty-five kilometres from town and the cattle markets. A school was only eight kilometres away and served by a bus. With three children enrolled in a correspondence school, and two more children approaching school age, a school was mandatory.

The problem was the price being three times the value of our ranch. How could we afford it? Perhaps if we had enough time, like twenty years or so...

Orville considered the possibilities. We didn't have enough cattle to make the payments. The ranch wasn't producing enough hay to feed enough cattle to make the payments. But Orville looked at the ranch's 4,000 acres and envisioned water from the higher country dramatically increasing their productivity to make the "not enough" enough.

He remembered the small flock of sheep he had tended as a boy. In his mind's eye he saw one mother ewe with two lambs being marketed for twice the ewe's value.

We sold our first ranch and most of our cattle and bought 700 ewes, and made a small down payment on the 144 Mile Ranch, which was priced at $30,000. To us in 1949, the price was a staggering amount.

FROM ROADHOUSE TO RANCH HOUSE

With the ranch came the roadhouse that had served in the 1860s as a stopping place for the miners and adventurers who were flocking to the booming gold rush town of Barkerville.

A road had been built from the port city of Vancouver, where the Fraser River meets the Pacific Ocean, up the awesome Fraser River Canyon. The road hung on trestles from the rock walls and twisted up side canyons and bridged tumultuous mountain streams. Up this road adventurers and dreamers came from everywhere heading for the fabulously rich gold fields of the Cariboo.

At first the Cariboo Trail began at Lillooet before the Fraser Canyon Trail was completed, winding through the dry hills and gulches and pushing northward through bogs and thick spruce forests to Barkerville.

To supply food and lodging to the travellers, roadhouses sprang up along the trail. They were named according to their distance from Lillooet, thus the 144 Mile Roadhouse.

By 1949 the character and faded glory of this old roadhouse still lingered. But as a ranch house and family home it left much to be desired. The upstairs bedrooms still had the numbers on the doors, one to six. They were small rooms each with one deep dormer window. They were hot in summer and cold in winter. The gable end, finished with rough boards with no insulation, was especially cold in winter.

It wasn't long before I was knocking out those walls between the bedrooms. It was one layer of boards running up and down and covered with aged, cracked wallpaper. It made one large, semi-divided, airier room for our three oldest girls. A few sheets of plywood were used to build stow-away spots, desks and closets under the eaves. They were rough but adequate from my point of view. Then some paper and paint and the stuffy little rooms became a comparatively pleasant larger room.

Some heavy felt paper to cover the rough boards on the gable end gave a bit of insulation. But if it hadn't been for the barrel heater in the lobby below, and the Klondike chimney running through the bedroom above, the occupants would have found those minus-forty-degree (or lower) nights even harder to endure.

Downstairs to the right of the lobby was a small bedroom that became our nursery. Behind it was a room that had been the family parlour. This became our bedroom.

Behind the lobby was the kitchen, bypassed by a short hall to the guests' long dining room. The kitchen was large enough to hold a table and benches to seat at least ten people. A big wood range and the wood box stood beside the entry door. Beside it was a stand for the wash basin and the water bucket, and the bane of my life, a slop pail for the wastewater. That kitchen was a thorn in my flesh. A door in the middle of every wall made it impossible to arrange any work area.

Roast Chicken Coming Up

When I was about twelve, my mother needed a little help with chicken dinner for guests the next day, and I gallantly volunteered, little suspecting what help would be required.

The first assignment was, "Go get that rooster in the pen and chop his head off."

Well! That wasn't the kind of help I had anticipated. But… "Can I shoot him with the .22 instead?" I anxiously inquired.

"Yeah, I guess so," Mother replied, hardly hearing me as she scurried about the kitchen.

I got the .22 rifle, loaded it and went to the pen that the rooster was in. I was familiar with .22s, having practised on targets under adult supervision. Well, there is the rooster. I stood by the pen, loaded rifle in hand, and carefully took aim at the rooster's head. The bullet went right through his head. "Cock-a-doodle-do," says he, "Cock-a-doodle-do," up and down went his head and "Cock-a-doodle-do," went he.

Spooked, I tried again. "Cock-a-doodle-do," says he again! I tried again and again. I presume I finally hit the very tiny bit of brain a rooster must have, and my chore was done.

Marie Fletcher holds her daughter, Iris, in front of her on the saddle while
heading out to check on cattle in the 150 Mile House area. Photo taken in 1939.

"Look, honey," I coaxed Orville for the umpteenth time. "If we moved that partition
back three or four feet I could have a work centre that would hold everything I need in
one place. The sink could go there."

"What sink?" Orville moved indifferently out the door. Ranchers are not usually
concerned with household matters.

A stove, a table, benches, a few shelves, a stand for the water bucket and basin, and
underneath, our disposal system—the obnoxious slop pail; this was a completely furnished kitchen. A wife who thought it was not adequate soon discovered there were more
important things to deal with.

One morning the boss rode off to attend to some of those more important things at
the far meadow, and didn't plan on returning for two or three days. He hadn't got out of
sight before I had a hammer and wrecking bar and was attacking that wall. It was only a
single layer of upright boards nailed to a board along the floor, and another along the ceiling. It wasn't long before I had the whole thing down.

Then I started putting those boards upright a few feet further over, and they were too
long. The old ceiling had sunk several inches where it earlier had been held up by the partition. I was contemplating how to deal with this problem when in the door walks the boss.

I can't remember all that he said. I guess that one's memory is sometimes mercifully blank. However, the remarks ended with "Well-l-l where do you want it?"

I gratefully said, "About here," and held the boards in place while he measured and sawed and grumbled.

The next day he was again off to attend to those things, having asked as he gave me a good-bye hug, "Would you change the turn-outs on the irrigation in the Spring Field?"

Marie Fletcher drives a team of horses pulling a hay slip of fresh hay to the barn.

Having attended to that chore, I proceeded to build counters and shelving. I was quite pleased with my arrangement even if it didn't have doors or arborite top. After a good paint job, it looked all right to me.

Later we found a dandy old cast-iron enameled sink. It even had double drain boards. True it didn't yet have taps or drains, but the horrid old slop pail had a hiding place even if it did sometimes get forgotten and overflowed.

In due time the water did come from taps and ran out drains, and the little path to the four-seater outhouse, the relic of the gold rush days, grew dim. The long dining room became a bedroom, a bathroom, and next to the kitchen, a laundry room, which replaced a laundry shed that used to freeze up every winter.

The old roadhouse that had served the travellers in the gold rush days of the 1860s had taken on a new character in the 1950s and had become a home.

EDITOR'S NOTE

The last two sections of Marie Fletcher's story, "The 144 Mile Ranch" and "From Roadhouse to Ranch House," came from her autobiography, *In Time—A Ranch*, self-published by Trafford Publishing in 2003.

The Dickinson Sisters

BY GLORIA ATAMANENKO
WITH ANNE PORTER & FAYE LUTZ

The Great Depression of the 1930s brought newcomers to the Cariboo in search of work and economic opportunities. Among them were Eve and Joy Dickinson, two young women in their early twenties from the Greater Vancouver area now known as Haney. Their mother had died, and in 1935 they had to seek employment. There was no work to be found in the Lower Mainland, so they responded to an advertisement for work on a ranch in the West Chilcotin. They were accepted, and left their urban home, little realizing that they would spend the rest of their long lives in that beautiful, remote rural area.

Their first job was working together at the ranch and miners' camp of K.B. Moore in Tatlayoko Valley. As they became acquainted with the community they went on to take other jobs. Eve was hired to teach the eight- and nine-year-old daughters of Harry and Amelia McGhee, Katie and Helen, who lived at the ranch next door to K.B. Moore—too far from the little school at Tatla Lake. Her teaching made education possible for children who would not have obtained it otherwise.

Joy went to work for Mrs. Bob Graham of Tatla Lake, the major stopping place in the West Chilcotin at that time. Living and working at the Grahams gave Joy the

Eve Chignell stands beside her father, James Dickenson, on the right. On the left Eve's husband Tom Chignell holds their youngest daughter, Ruth. The other children are Nancy Chignell, Jim Eastabrook and Roy Graham. The vehicle in the background is Tom Chignell's camperized truck he used as his home away from home while maintaining the phone line from Tatla Lake to the Bella Coola Hill.

opportunity to meet various residents of the Chilcotin, and to gain insight into their lives and struggles in challenging times.

In 1938, Eve married Tom Chignell, West Chilcotin's telephone lineman, whose diligent, demanding work kept the widely scattered residents of the area in touch with one another and with the world outside.

In 1939, Joy married the Grahams' eldest son, Bill. Her new baby niece, Faye, was baptized on her Aunt Joy's wedding day.

Bill Graham was a brilliant, self-taught mechanic whose knowledge of machinery and skills in road building and maintenance was in constant demand. His work required much travelling and Joy often travelled with him. Described by her daughter Anne as a terrific cook, Joy often did the cooking in the temporary work camps. At other times, she brought boxes of food she had prepared at home for the work crews. A capable amateur photographer, Joy often took photos of the workers and their working conditions, adding to the photographic records of Chilcotin history.

Hired to run Bill Graham's Cat, Alf Bracewell bulldozed the road from Anahim Lake to Bella Coola down the infamous, formidable "Hill" in 1953, to meet George

Dalshaug bulldozing from the bottom of the Hill, starting a new phase in the vast region's history. Over the next years (and to some extent continuing into the present time) there was still much improvement and maintenance to be done. One summer, Bill Graham worked on the road himself, and Joy and little daughter Anne camped with him. Joy cooked for the crew and witnessed the difficulties and dangers the workers faced maintaining a road in an extremely challenging mountain environment.

Since childhood, Joy Graham had always been interested in history. Living in the West Chilcotin during a time of many major changes made a deep impression on her. She believed that the historic heritage of this vast, beautiful area should be recognized, recorded, and conserved. She saved and collected artifacts with heritage significance. With other interested full-time and part-time residents of the West Chilcotin, she helped to found the West Chilcotin Museum and Historical Society.

The goals of the Society include the conservation and celebration of the various aspects of West Chilcotin history, and, in time, to establish a museum at Tatla Lake. Until a museum is established, Joy's collection, and those of other participants, is held in trust by the Museum of the Cariboo-Chilcotin in Williams Lake.

Close family ties and her love of the country helped Joy to stay connected to the West Chilcotin even when age and health made it necessary for her to live in Williams Lake. She loved to go back to Tatla Lake to visit her family, and joked about applying a lead foot to the gas pedal to drive there faster!

Joy Graham's clarity of vision and gentle but determined perseverance are a lasting inspiration to the members of the society she founded.

ABOVE: Joy Graham, left, with daughter Anne, and Joy's twin sister, Dot Eastabrook, do some shopping in Vancouver, 1956.

OPPOSITE BOTTOM: A hay crew at the Graham Ranch in Tatla Lake take a well-deserved break for lunch after putting in long, hot hours harvesting the hay crop.

OPPOSITE TOP: Joy Graham sits in the tent at one of the many road camps she shared over the years with her husband Bill, left, as he worked his bulldozer building roads in the West Chilcotin. Visiting the Grahams is friend, Doreen, right.

Ingaborg Hansen

BY GLORIA ATAMANENKO
WITH BOB HOLM

This is a bouquet of memories of Ingaborg Hansen, who loved flowers so dearly, and who coped with the challenges of Chilcotin life and found ways of cheering it with grace and beauty.

Ingaborg Anna Lena was born on August 31, 1920, in Hamburg, Germany. Gifted with a beautiful, deep contralto voice, she became a singer with a small opera company. They toured Northern Germany, and also entertained troops during the war years. In 1955 she came to Canada to marry Tex Hansen, and arrived at Clearwater Lake in the West Chilcotin on October 4. The following morning, six inches of new snow covered the ground. It delighted their little son Bobby, who grew to love trapping in winter and fishing in summer. To Ingaborg it was an introduction to the harsh winters of the Chilcotin and the hard work ahead.

The first five years were very difficult for Ingaborg and Tex. There were fences to build, necessitating miles of walking through deep snow to find trees slender enough for fence posts and rails. There were guest cabins to build and furnish, and cattle and horses to feed and water through a long winter.

In springtime there was a garden to create in lean soil and a limited growing season. In raised beds with plastic covers, Ingaborg managed to grow strawberries, peas, and beans. In the regular garden, enough cabbage and hardier root vegetables (parsnips, turnips, carrots, etc.) were grown to store in the root cellar for the winter. There was poultry to raise for eggs and meat, including chickens, turkeys, ducks, and geese. In summertime, there was haying to help with. She pitched hay and did whatever else was needed. There was no outdoor work that Ingaborg was not willing to do.

For guests it was Ingaborg's work as a homemaker that was the most apparent and appreciated. A planter brimming with pansies welcomed visitors at the front door. Inside, the pioneer starkness of the log cabin was softened by billowing lace curtains in the windows, pictures on the walls, a white tablecloth, and beautiful china gracing the table. Recorded music recalled a continent far away. And oh, the marvelous smell and taste of Ingaborg's cooking and baking. There was homemade bread, biscuits, and Danish pastries (which Danish-born Tex especially appreciated). There was roasted goose, fluffy mashed potatoes, moose salami and brandied peaches.

Ingaborg made wine also. Rhubarb was plentiful and was turned into many delicacies, including wine. Wild soapallalie berries with their sharp taste yielded a beautiful amber coloured wine which "kicked like a mule!" Later, as time and budget allowed, there were peach and plum wines as well.

Ingaborg and Tex were neighbourly people, and always helpful in times of need. Stranded travellers were always welcomed in, fed, and housed. Guests came from all over Canada, Europe, and the US Summer work crews also appreciated Ingaborg's excellent meals. Tex and Ingaborg were warm, welcoming, generous hosts. At Christmas-time, the great spruce tree in their living room, dec-

"A planter brimming with pansies welcomed visitors at the door."

— GLORIA ATAMANENKO

Ingaborg Hansen, left, stands in front of her home at Clearwater Lake with neighbour and Kleena Kleene school teacher Ginty Paul.

orated only with white candles, was the essence of Christmas beauty and joy. When saying goodbye to departing friends, Ingaborg stood outside and waved with both arms, like a hug for the road.

Age and health necessitated a move from the Chilcotin to Vancouver Island. Delicate roses, rhododendrons, and fruit trees at Cobble Hill replaced the pansies, rhubarb, and soapallalies of the West Chilcotin. The Women's Farm Institute at Cobble Hill enjoyed Ingaborg's energy and hospitality, and the knowledge, which she was always willing to share with others.

Ingaborg spent the last year of her life in Powell River close to her family, including Bob, Diana, Ryan, and Jessica Holm. In June 2003, she was laid to rest at Cobble Hill Cemetery beside her love, Tex Hansen.

Lena Jack

BY SAGE BIRCHWATER

Lena Jack relaxes in her living room after a day of puttering in her garden at Dog Creek. She turned ninety years old in 2008, and is the oldest member of the Canoe Creek/Dog Creek First Nation still living in the community. She says she's always had a garden and it's a way of life that keeps her young.

"I grow all the vegetables: onions, carrots, turnips, Swiss chard, beans, lettuce, tomatoes, corn, cantaloupe, and potatoes. At one time my mother and I used to plant four one-hundred-pound sacks of seed potatoes." She also grows currants, strawberries and rhubarb.

Lena has had several garden sites over the years. Down along the Fraser River at Spring Gulch she used to grow hundreds of pounds of potatoes. Other community members grew potatoes there too. The climate is too hot to live there but there is a good source of water, she says.

"Whoever was passing by would irrigate the potatoes. When someone went down salmon fishing they would water the garden." Lena also had a garden with two of her sisters-in-law, Seraphine and Celestine, at Canoe Lake. She had ten children to feed, and depended on her garden to provide food for them. She and her husband Francis Camille worked together canning the vegetables and fruit from their garden along with wild berries they harvested from the land. They also dried and canned salmon, trout, moose and deer meat.

Lena Jack is surrounded by her family who she nurtured and encouraged to succeed in school. Daughter Agness Jack, right, and granddaughters Barb Morin, left, and Phyllis Webstad have all benefited from Lena's striving for excellence.

"I tanned hides and did buckskin gloves, vests, jackets and moccasins," she says. "We dried sxusem (soap berries) and saskatoons. When there were no jars long ago, we used to cut the necks off the bottles to do our canning." She also gathered plants for medicine for her children and even today advises which plants to use for various ailments.

Lena was born in Dog Creek in 1918. Her mother, Susan Edwards Jim, from nearby Canoe Creek, told stories of the times before the Churn Creek suspension bridge was built over the Fraser River in 1913. Lena remembers her father, George Jim, building a pit house up at their place near T'sepetn' (Gustafsen Lake area). "Many people lived there, it was a good place for hunting, trapping, fishing and gathering," she says. "Before I was born, there was no bridge over the Fraser River. There were cabins down by the river and a guy used to bring people across the river in a scow. The cows and horses had to swim across."

In the fall, people would cross the river on the scow and head out on the west side of the Fraser to go hunting and trapping. When they returned in December they often had to camp at Churn Creek to wait for the river to freeze so they could walk back across on the ice to come home.

In 1925, Lena was sent to St. Joseph's Mission near Williams Lake. "I went to school there for ten years," she says. "Our grades only went up to grade eight, then they let us out." At the Mission she says academic subjects were taught only half the day. The rest of the time the children had to work. Lena learned to read and write and speak English well, and she also learned how to sew and knit and play the harmonica.

"We did all the work when we were in school," she recalls. "We did our laundry, cleaned the convent, cleaned the kitchen, baked bread, mended our clothes, made new clothes, and made butter." She says the residential school was called an industrial school in those days. Its intent was to prepare aboriginal children to take jobs in the labour force. "I always cried when I had to go to the Mission. They took us away in September and let us out in July. We used to come home in August."

Lena's own children and some of her grandchildren went to the Mission as well. "Three generations of us went there," says her daughter Agness Jack. "When I was there it seemed like we were always praying. For me going to church was an escape because then they left you alone. It was one of my survival skills. I could be in one place reciting prayers but my mind was elsewhere." Agness says when her niece Phyllis went to the Mission it wasn't so heavily Catholic. By then the Mission was just a residence for native children and they were bused to public schools in Williams Lake and 150 Mile House.

In 2008 Lena had thirty-six grandchildren and great-grandchildren. There was a five-generation line that included Lena, her daughter Rose, Rose's daughter Phyllis, Phyllis' son Jeremy, and Jeremy's son Blake.

The topography of Dog Creek on a fertile bench above the Fraser River provides a wide range of climatic types that the Secwepemc people learned to take advantage of over the centuries they occupied the territory. From the headwaters of Dog Creek in the high plateau hill country south and west of Lac la Hache, the water flows west in a gentle decline to the lower elevation, broadening out into a fertile valley that buttresses up against the semi-arid grasslands of the Fraser River canyon. It is here, in Dog Creek Valley, that most of the people live.

The community of Dog Creek has historical roots that extend back to the Cariboo Gold Rush days of the 1860s. The original Cariboo Gold Rush Trail from Lillooet to Barkerville followed the east side of the Fraser River from Pavilion to Jesmond via Kelly Lake and on to Canoe Creek, Dog Creek and Alkali Lake. When the cattle industry got started in the Chilcotin in the late 1800s, the main route to supply these ranches from the railhead at Ashcroft crossed the Fraser River below Dog Creek.

The headwaters of Dog Creek are more temperate and moist than the scorching desert along the Fraser. The country south of Lac la Hache is dotted with small lakes full of fish, with an abundance of wild hay meadows scattered through the pine and fir forests. "That was the bread basket for the community," Agness says, noting that one of the largest of these lakes is the man-made Gustafson Lake, which the Dog Creek people call Big Lake or T'sepet'n. The big earth dam at the lake's outflow was created by horse-drawn scoops to excavate the necessary fill. The lake is an important reservoir for the Dog Creek watershed. Like many Canoe Creek/Dog Creek families, Lena's parents had a meadow, barns and corrals in this upper country, and rafts on various lakes to set a net to catch fish. In the winter they trapped and hunted in the forest of this region.

Pithouses were still in use when Lena was young. Archeological work analyzing the fill used to build the T'sepet'n (Gustafson Lake) dam shows extensive evidence of early habitation. "Our people used pithouses and lived all over," Lena says. "My dad built one of those houses in 1935. It was 1940 before he built a log cabin at T'sepet'n. He had some-body helping him build it."

She says when she was growing up, people were always busy fishing, hunting, pick-ing berries, or working for cash by cowboying, fencing or haying for the various ranches. "They didn't have no welfare in those days, so we had to work hard."

Lac la Hache was a key intertribal trading site for the Secwepemc, Tsilhqot'in and Dakelh (Carrier) who would gather there to socialize and exchange items of commerce. "It's one of two areas where our people gathered to trade and barter," says Agness.

Lena is proud she didn't lose her language. Though speaking Shuswap was strictly forbidden at the Mission and children were severely punished if they were caught using their native language, Lena says she spoke it anyway, quietly to her friends. Agness finds it ironic that while the aboriginal children weren't allowed to speak their native languages at the Mission, the priests and nuns who hailed from France, often spoke French.

Lena has been an avid reader all her life. She says she found one piece of Cariboo history a bit ironic. "They called us savages, yet in a book I read, people who had money stayed in a hotel along the Cariboo Road, and the women who owned the roadhouse used to kill them and throw them in a lake and steal their money."

As the matriarch of a large extended family, Lena has always encouraged her eight children and now more than forty grandchildren to get an education.

"Mom was very thoughtful," says Agness. "She would buy us cards of encouragement and send them to us when we were away at school. Even at university." She says her dad talked some sense to her one time as well. "When I wanted to quit school in grade eight, my dad gave me one of his infamous long lectures. He said I had a couple of choices. He said I could stay at Dog Creek and marry a dropout or go to work for very little money somewhere." Agness took her father's words to heart and stayed in school and graduated with a degree from university.

Lena says the key to staying healthy is "be active." At ninety years old she was up early tending her garden or doing something. One of her grandchildren commented one time that when he and his mother went to bed, Lena was sitting in a chair sewing. When he woke up in the morning, Lena was sitting in the same chair still sewing. "You know Granny, me and Mommy went to bed," he told her.

There's longevity in Lena's family. Her mother lived to 110. "Mom loves to dance," Agness says. "She does the Irish jig. She outlasts us, and tires us out."

"I've seen my fifth generation," Lena says.

EDITOR'S NOTE: This article appeared in *Casual Country*, 2007.

Maddie Jack

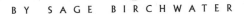

BY SAGE BIRCHWATER

When Maddie Jack was born in the remote Ulkatcho country north of Anahim Lake in 1929, the landscape of British Columbia looked a lot different than it does today. Never mind the mountain pine beetle epidemic that got its start in the late 1990s in Tweedsmuir Park just west of where she was born, and swept across the province to the Rocky Mountains and beyond. And never mind the ever-persistent building of roads in the West Chilcotin beginning in the 1980s that seriously transformed the tone of untouched wilderness.

When Maddie was born, the Ootsa Lake reservoir had not been created yet. The building of the Kenny Dam across the Nechako River in 1953 created a water barrier that cut off the natural travel route used by the Ulkatcho people to visit their neighbours in Chezlatta. When she was about twelve years old Maddie went with her uncle Lassis West to Burns Lake by horse and sleigh from her home in Ulkatcho Village (eighty kilometres north of Anahim Lake), to celebrate Christmas Mass with the priest at Chezlatta. Ulkatcho people commonly visited relatives in Chezlatta in those days by swimming their horses across the Nechako River or taking their horse-drawn sleighs over the ice in winter.

In the 1930s and '40s Ulkatcho Village lay in the centre of a vast unroaded expanse.

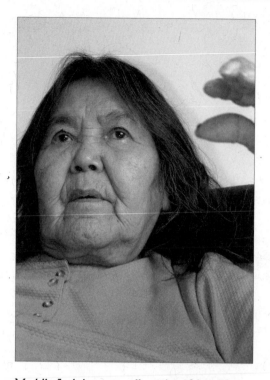

Maddie Jack loves to tell stories of her life growing up in the country around Ulkatcho Village, about eighty kilometres north of Anahim Lake. There she travelled great distances by horseback with her grandparents.

Throughout the year people travelled by saddle horse and pack horse or by foot on the network of trails that linked the Fraser River to the Central Coast. In the winter when the wetlands froze and were covered with a blanket of snow, horse-drawn sleighs were the easiest way to transport bulk supplies of goods.

Ulkatcho Village lies on the ancient Nuxalk-Carrier Grease Trail that Alexander Mackenzie followed on his famous trek across North America in 1793. Mackenzie noted in his journal the great Culla Culla longhouse located at the village. According to ethnographers this vestige of coastal culture so far inland, indicated the strong bond of friendship that existed between the people of Ulkatcho and the tribes of the Nuxalk and Kimsquit of the Central Coast. Ulkatcho Village was a major trading centre between the Interior and Coastal First Nations people.

The Ulkatcho families have always been great travellers. They had to cover large distances to hunt and gather enough resources to sustain themselves. It wasn't uncommon to journey 300 kilometres east to the Fraser River or 200 kilometres west to Kimsquit and Bella Coola in a single year.

"My parents died pretty young," Maddie says. "I was ten when my mom, Panny, died, and my dad got shot when I was three."

So Maddie and her brother Pierre (P.L.) West were raised by both sets of their grandparents, Charlie and Jeanie West, and Captain Harry and O'Christine.

"Every year we went to Bella Coola with Charlie West and Jeanie. We worked on the hay down there and in the gardens digging potatoes. We went there by horseback past Tanya Lakes on the Mackenzie Trail."

Ulkatcho Village was so remote that Maddie never had to attend residential school like many other First Nations children did. Instead she attended school for two years at Ulkatcho Village, when the Department of Indian Affairs managed to convince a teacher to open up a school there in the early 1940s.

"But they can't have a school down there at Ulkatcho," Maddie says. "Two years they tried it, but the teacher said the water no good." So that plan got abandoned.

Most of the Ulkatcho families had their own meadows, homesteads and traplines in the country surrounding Ulkatcho Village, and most families had a house at Ulkatcho Village as well. "Grampa Charlie West had a house down at Mud Lake or Tsilbisko. Captain Harry and my grandma O'Christine had a house downriver past Majuba."

Families gathered at Ulkatcho Village for special occasions like Christmas or when the Oblate priest Father Francois Marie Thomas arrived for Priest Time in June.

Maddie describes travelling with the seasons. "In July a lot of people stay at Tanya Lakes to make dried fish. They had three smokehouses over there. We stayed in Bella Coola until haying time then we come back and make our own hay at Mud Lake in the first of August. Then we go back down the mountain to Bella Coola after that to dig potatoes."

Then it was home again to go trapping at Mud Lake for the winter. "We mostly travelled with pack horses," says Maddie. "Six horses for the four of us. One time Grampa's horse died on him at the top of the mountain. A plant that looks like a corn tree (Indian hellebore); horse eat it and die right now."

Maddie said she heard the horse holler and went out to see what the matter was. "I go out and look and the horse is lying there. I told Grandma and she says he's dead. Lots of people's horse died that way. Eat those things and he's dead. Poison."

She says people had to tie their horses up to keep them from eating the deadly hellebore plants. "Grampa had to walk home. Next year he took another horse."

One thing Maddie says Ulkatcho people learned, was not to buy horses raised in Bella Coola and bring them to the high plateau country. Coastal horses were too soft and didn't have the stamina or know-how to rustle through the snow over the long winter, she says. "Take him home he die on you. Never be alive, he's dead. Better to get a horse from the Chilcotin."

> *"One time Grampa's horse died at the top of the mountain."*
>
> — MADDIE JACK

One reason for the good relations between the Ulkatcho and Nuxalk people was the intermarrying that occurred between the two communities. "My grampa, Charlie West, his mom comes from Nuxalk. He can speak the Bella Coola language. They call my grampa Mucklehuse after one of the mountains in Bella Coola. It means his face is red like the setting sun shining on the mountain. The other mountain has a big bald head they call Squinas."

Maddie says she has lots of good friends among the Nuxalk people in Bella Coola. "Every time they see me they want to hug me. My friends and my cousins are down there."

Continuing her description of moving about with the seasons, Maddie says after a long winter of trapping down the river, her family would come up to Anahim Lake for the Stampede in early July. After the Stampede they would head down to Bella Coola on the trails through the Precipice Valley.

"People in Precipice look after the telephone all the time. Then after fishing and picking berries down there we would come back up the Grease Trail, Grampa called it the Mackenzie Road."

Maddie says her grandmother Jeanie West came from the Chilcotin country around Nemiah Valley. "Sometimes Grampa and Grandma go down there and dig wild potatoes, and bring some back."

When she was still a teenager Maddie married John Jack and the couple had two children, Annie and McKinnon. She says Annie was born at Ulkatcho Village in 1947. Her grandmother O'Christine was the midwife. McKinnon was born later in Chilliwack.

John and Maddie both trapped for a living and raised a small herd of beef cattle down the river from Anahim Lake. John logged for a time in Bella Coola and worked as a hunting guide over the years. "We sold our furs to Darcy Christensen. He used to fly out and pick up the furs and bring me some groceries. He landed on the ice. When Darcy bring me groceries sometimes he pick me up in Anahim Lake and fly me home. I give him a cow in fall time to pay off the bill."

Maddie has outlived her two children, Annie and McKinnon, and husband John, but she's surrounded by family in Anahim Lake. "I've got twelve grandchildren, ten great-grandchildren, and two great-great-grandchildren." On August 10, 2009, Maddie turned eighty years old.

EDITOR'S NOTE:
This article appeared in *Casual Country*, 2007.

Olive Lock MacKenzie

BY PAM MAHON

O live Lock MacKenzie is an inspiration to all who know her. At ninety-four years old she still cards and spins her own wool and tends a fairly large vegetable and flower garden at her home in Miocene. She keeps busy every second of the day knitting and hooking rugs, and gives away everything she makes to friends and family.

Olive is the only child of English parents. She was born on May 26, 1915, on her grandmother's farm in Devonshire, England. Her parents had immigrated to Canada in 1912, but returned to Devonshire to settle Olive's grandmother's estate and stayed there for eighteen months. It was during this time that Olive was born. They left for Canada again in August 1915, when Olive was ten weeks old, and they came straight to 153 Mile House where an uncle owned Clark's Meadow.

The family put up some hay and spent their first winter in a one-room, sod-roofed cabin so overrun with packrats that her father, Bill Lock, sat up at night with a .22 rifle and flashlight to shoot them as they ran along the centre beam. During that winter, Bill took up a section of land to the south, and cut logs for fencing and a new cabin. In 1916 they moved in. Olive's mother thought it was a great improvement. Although it too had a sod roof, it had the added bonus of a puncheon floor made of split logs. Over the next two years they built a small log house, a barn, and corrals.

 *Spring of 2002*

O' peein' in the snow,
An' lookin' down the hole,
It's the closest thing to grass I'm gonna see.

The wind, she sure does blow,
The trees are rockin' to and fro,
While the eagles, they soar so bold and free.

The temperature has been so bitter cold,
Squirrel towin' the robin to make 'em go,
They say, "it's global warming, that's the key."

You'd never know that it's May,
And, the 9th day, by the way.
This must be some kinda' record by quite a few degrees.

Oh, it's the sixth day in a row,
That it's been hoverin' down below.
If it's spring you want to see, take your luck with two o' three.

The hay is getting really low
And I'm running out of dough.
My banker I have to see, or maybe win the lottery.

The cows have just been polled,
"Let's put our calves all on hold.
It's a whole lot warmer here inside of me."

Ground's too cold for seeds to grow,
So I guess there will be no rows to hoe,
Guess we'll havta join the beetles dining on yon' pine tree.

There will be no hay to mow,
And there will be no bales to throw,
So there'll be lots of time for fishin' for you and me.

O' peein' in the snow,
An' lookin' down the hole,
It's the closest thing to grass I'm gonna see.

— Olive Lock MacKenzie

Olive Lock MacKenzie rides in a horse-drawn carriage as the guest of honour in the Williams Lake Stampede Parade. At ninety-four years old in 2009 she still tends her large flower and vegetable garden in Miocene, and stays busy spinning wool and knitting items for her family.

Though she had no other kids to play with, Olive says she wasn't lonely. Her constant companion and entertainment was a white horse named Dick that she rode bareback with a piece of rope around his neck. Although she was only three or four at the time, she would pull him over to the fence by the rope and climb on. She also had a little black dog who was so loyal that it would pick up her woollen hat whenever it fell off on a winter sleigh trip to 153 Mile and carry it for a long way.

School didn't start for Olive until she was nearly nine, once her parents figured she was old enough to make the one-hour horseback ride to the school. By that time her horse was a black mare named Queenie, who was an unwanted foal, but turned out to be a great horse.

Olive entered Queenie in the children's race at the Williams Lake Stampede and won so easily that it was suggested she enter the ladies' race. She won that, too, and Olive raced on Queenie many times, always riding bareback. Queenie was only ever beaten by a thoroughbred.

In 1927, at the age of twelve, Olive and Queenie won a beautiful silver cup. After that Olive started riding racehorses for local horse racing promoter, Jimmy Smith, and she learned to use a racing saddle. She did that until she was eighteen when, sadly, Jimmy Smith died.

Olive always helped on the ranch, driving the mower for haying and doing other chores. When her dad bought a new buck rake, he didn't have time to set it up and see how it worked, so Olive figured it out, harnessed the team, and it became her job. She was only thirteen.

She first saw her future husband, Bill MacKenzie, when she was fourteen and he was seventeen and working at the garage at 150 Mile House. She says they probably met formally at the school Christmas dance.

"She gives away everything she makes."

— PAM MAHON

Olive and Bill were married on February 2, 1937, and spent the first year with her parents. Their oldest daughter, Myrtle, was born in November of that year.

Bill took a job in Ucluelet on Vancouver Island to build a large hangar and made enough money to buy sixty acres of land at Rose Lake. Then he started working at the Bullion Mine at Likely, so they sold the sixty acres at Rose Lake, and after their second child, Gordon, was born, they moved back to Olive's parents' ranch again.

In 1941 the Shadbolt place came up for sale for $2,000 and they paid $200 annually for ten years. When they moved to the Shadbolt place they had ten cows, and bought eight or nine more from the Shadbolts. There were two sets of twins from these cows, which they considered a good omen for their ranch. Mr. Shadbolt said that in all his years of ranching he had never had a set of twin calves.

They had up to eighty-nine ewes for a while, but losses to coyote and lynx were too high, so they sold them. Olive remembers some sheep belonging to a neighbour showing up, and he came to collect them with a flat-deck truck with a rail down the centre. He tied the fifteen sheep to either side of the rail and set off home with them standing peacefully for the ride.

In the following years three more children were born, Shirley, Kenny, and Cathy. As it was a long way for them to go to school at Rose Lake, Bill and Olive pre-empted property nearer the Horsefly Road and built a two-storey house, which they moved into in 1950. Bill also built a barn, and with his brother Jack, built a log cabin for their mother when she came to stay.

The family bought a cabin at Mitchell Bay in 1969, where the road was never plowed in winter. They used snowmobiles and a toboggan to get in there. Once the road was kept plowed, Olive would snowshoe in to check the cabin in the winter and shovel the snow off the roof.

When they were both in their sixties, Bill and Olive sold their ranch to their daughter Cathy and continued to live on the property and help out with the ranch activities. After Bill passed away, Olive remained in her rural home, keeping her large garden with a lovely show of flowers and vegetables. She collects all her own seeds.

Olive was always interested in working with wool, and has had a spinning wheel since 1943. She traded a saddle blanket for it, and it was delivered on a sleigh with a set of farming disks, somewhat the worse for wear. However, she got it going and learned to spin. Recently she designed and made new bobbins for it.

Life is always busy for Olive, making socks, sweaters, and vests for her many grand- and great-grandchildren; canning, pickling, or freezing the produce from her garden; making frames for neighbours who want to hook their own saddle pads or seat pads; or just acting as host to her many friends and relations.

She celebrated her ninetieth birthday in style in the summer of 2005 at the Miocene Community Hall, which she and Bill helped to build thirty years earlier.

Chiwid

BY SAGE BIRCHWATER

Lilly Skinner, better known as Chiwid, is an inspiration for women dealing with personal adversity. According to baptismal records, she was born in the summer of 1903, to Lausap, a Tsilhqot'in woman, who was deaf and mute, and had to "speak on her hands." It was conveyed to Father Francois Marie Thomas during Priest Time at Redstone Flats in June 1904, that the father of eleven-month-old Chiwid was a white man, Charlie Skinner, who raised horses in the Eagle Lake country between Tatlayoko Valley and the Chilko River, north of the Potato Mountains. So she was given the last name, Skinner.

There were few white settlers in the Chilcotin in those days. People made their living trapping animals for fur, trading and packing, and digging the ground for gold and other minerals. In the early 1900s cattle ranching started pushing its way westward into the upper reaches of the Chilcotin River watershed.

Tsilhqot'in people lived a mobile existence across the length and breadth of the Chilcotin Plateau in those days, from the Bella Coola Valley to the Fraser River. They moved about the land throughout the year hunting, fishing and gathering resources with the seasons. Chiwid grew up with half a dozen different siblings born to her mother, all fathered by different white men, and raised by different members of her extended family.

Chiwid stands by one of her brush houses near Tatla Lake where she stayed all winter, despite temperatures sometimes dropping to fifty below zero. PHOTO JOY GRAHAM

"First time I see Chiwid, she was a young girl, a little bit older than me," recalled Lucy Sulin of Towdystan. "At Clearwater Lake, where they were trapping fish where the creek goes out of the lake. I remember Chiwid's uncle, Little Johnny, looking for her. He had a big stick because Chiwid run off with some boys. Little Johnny raised Chiwid. Her mother Lausap was deaf and couldn't speak."

Chiwid was still a teenager when she gave birth to two daughters, Cecilia and Julianna. At some point she married Alec Jack, a Tsilhqot'in man from Nemiah Valley, but according to Julianna, Alec Jack wasn't her or her sister's biological father. Instead, she said, that distinction went to Bob Graham, the owner of Tatla Lake Ranch. But Alec Jack raised the girls as his own.

Chiwid is described as a very beautiful woman. Chezacut rancher, Randolph Mulvahill, said she was one of those women who didn't have to do anything to look good. "She could have been all mud and dirt out of the gutter, and she was still good looking," he said. "You see the odd person like that, and she was one of them."

Gerry Bracewell of Tatlayoko Valley also marvelled at her beauty. "I remember how

EDITOR'S NOTE:

In the interviews in this story the speaker often switches pronouns when talking about Chiwid. Prior to other cultures coming into the Chilcotin area, men and women were considered equal. The Tsilhqot'in language has no gender pronouns.

beautiful she was. All by herself with long black hair as shiny as a raven's wing. She was just there in the wilderness."

By the early 1930s Chiwid and Alec were living at Nimpo Lake Meadow. Their daughters, like most aboriginal children, were attending residential school 300 kilometres away at St. Joseph's Mission near Williams Lake. Late one winter a tragic incident occurred. Nobody knew for sure what brought it on, but word got out in early March that Alec Jack had beaten his wife to the point of death using a logging chain.

"Chiwid was a sweet person. Very nice looking and very kind."

— ALICE ENGEBRETSON

According to Alice Engebretson, the beating wasn't an isolated incident. Alice and her family had been living at the Engebretson ranch house at Towdystan for seven years and her parents and the Jacks were good friends.

"I was about ten years old when I first met Chiwid," Alice recalled. "She was a sweet person. Very nice looking and very kind. She used to stay with my parents while her husband was off chasing coyotes and wild horses with my dad."

Alice remembers Alec Jack as a very violent man. Especially with horses.

"Scotty Gregg (Lilly's half-brother) said Alec Jack was the meanest man he had ever seen. He said he especially didn't like anything that was female."

Alice said the domestic violence between Alec Jack and Chiwid was fueled by alcohol.

"Alec Jack made homebrew, then the beatings would start."

Alice's younger sister, Illa Graham, had her own memories of those times. "Chiwid was bright when I first knew her, but her husband used to beat her up so much she got mental. Alec Jack was always beating her up. They'd get to drinking or whatever and he'd get into a tantrum over a cow dying or something, and would go on a rampage."

Illa said her dad would go down and see if he could stop Alec from beating her up so bad. "Ollie Nukalow, Chiwid's half-brother, was only a kid of fourteen or fifteen at the time. He'd ride over and get my dad. Then dad would have to ride over to Nimpo Lake to quiet old Alec down."

Things were never the same for Chiwid and Alec Jack after that terrible beating in March 1933. When she returned to the Chilcotin after receiving medical treatment in Vancouver, Chiwid refused to live with Alec Jack any longer. Thus began her fifty-year reclusive existence living outside throughout the year, shunning the company of others and the comforts of living indoors, even during the extremes of the frigid Chilcotin winters where temperatures sometimes dipped lower than fifty below zero.

Chiwid uses two walking sticks to steady herself as she visits her neighbour, Veera Bonner, at Fletcher Lake near Big Creek. Chiwid's daughter Julianna Setah lived in the area and Chiwid camped outside nearby. PHOTO VEERA BONNER

Over those five decades Chiwid became a legend among her people and the hardy settlers who hacked out an existence on the Chilcotin Plateau.

Two years after beginning her solitary existence, Chiwid had another child, a daughter, Mary Jane. There was considerable speculation among the locals over who the father might be. A general consensus suggests it was Thomas Squinas, an Ulkatcho rancher living at Anahim Lake.

Chiwid raised Mary Jane on her own, demanding the same rigors of existence as she imposed on herself.

There are some stories about that too. Edward Sill, an Ulkatcho man, born in the country north of Anahim Lake, was brought to live with his half-brother Eagle Lake Henry near Henry's Crossing by the Chilko River when he was twelve years old. He recalled how Chiwid tethered Mary Jane to a stake at her isolated camp so she didn't run off and get lost. "When Mary Jane was a little kid Chiwid take him to Anahim Lake Stampede. Somebody ask him, 'what you do with your daughter?' He say, 'I tie him up in the camp.' Just like a dog he tie him up in the camp. He said he leave some water with him and tie him up in the camp. Mary Jane was just a kid."

Willie Sulin, a Tsilhqot'in man from Towdystan, who speculated it might have been he who fathered Mary Jane, came across the little girl alone in Chiwid's camp. "One time, just the other side, I found Lilly's kid, Mary Jane. He was about two years old. I guess Lilly's horse took off, and he went to look for it. That kid he go to sleep right there. Where one road goes through. The kid was there.

'Hey kid,' I told him.

'Mommy took off,' he said. 'He chase the horse.'

There was a blanket right there, and the kid had been sleeping. So, I took off, and after a while I found Lilly way up top of the hill.

'I lost my horse,' he say.

'I can get it for you,' I tell him. 'Go back to your daughter.'

Not too long I found the horse in a meadow, just behind the hill. I led the horse down, back to Lilly's camp. Lilly wasn't there yet, but that kid was still there, asleep on top of the blanket. I don't think Lilly was crazy. All his life he was like that."

Randolph Mulvahill was born and raised in Chezacut country. One day he was out hunting horses on the mountain by Chezacut Lake and thought he heard a child crying. "I was positive it was a kid crying. My horse was nervous because he didn't know what it was. He tossed his head and rolled the bit in his mouth. Finally I had to get off him to quiet him down. Sure enough, I could hear a kid crying."

Randolph says he thought it was strange and jumped back on his horse and rode towards the sound. "I saw horse tracks on the trail, and little kid tracks," he said. "As soon as the kid sees me, it let out a hell of a shriek and crawled under a log. Well what the hell are you going to do? The horse I was riding was green and not that well broke to pack a kid on, so I thought the best thing to do was not to do anything."

Randolph kept following the horse tracks and caught up with Chiwid, leading a saddle horse and three pack horses. After telling Chiwid the little girl was crying and he was kind of worried about her, Chiwid shrugged. "All the time he do that way. He cry and cry. After a while he come."

When Mary Jane got to be four or five years old she was adopted by a family from Anaham. Josephine Gregg said Chiwid took care of Mary Jane until she was old enough to go to school. "He was too mean to that little girl. Father Hennessy was the teacher at Redbrush. He saw her chase that girl around with a pitchfork, and told the cops or somebody. Then they take the kid away."

Alice Engebretson remembered that Mary Jane was born at the old Lester Dorsey place, in a tent under a spruce tree. "It was the year after Dave Dorsey was born. Jane Lehman attended the birth, and all the men were teasing about whose baby it was. Mrs. Bryant gave the baby milk and everything, and a few years later Jane eventually took the child away from Chiwid because there were reports she was starving it. She kept the baby for two months because it had malnutrition. That little girl was just skin and bones, but she was very good natured. She wouldn't cry about anything. The little girl stayed outside with Chiwid. When she was old enough to go to school, they sent her to St. Joseph's Mission near Williams Lake. She was adopted by a family from Anaham Reserve."

Once she no longer had Mary Jane to look after, Chiwid rarely put up her tent. Instead she'd camp under a tarp or a lean-to, or under a brushy tree.

Charlie Quilt recalled how one winter some folks went to look for Chiwid at her camp and couldn't see her anywhere. "There was a couple of feet of snow on the ground, but no fire, no nothing. No sign of life. They were just about to go when the snow cracked in front of them. Chiwid pushed the snow off her blanket and stood up. There was one log laying there, and she was laying down beside it, buried under the snow."

There was a certain pattern to Chiwid's existence as she travelled about the country living her outdoor solitary life. For the first few years she lived in the Anahim Lake area, not far from where she and Alec Jack had lived

Ulkatcho rancher, wolf hunter and trapper, Thomas Squinas, is thought to be the father of Chiwid's third daughter, Mary Jane. Standing with Thomas is Darcy Christensen holding the first coyote he ever trapped.
DARCY CHRISTENSEN COLLECTION

together. For one thing, she had family in the area. Her mother Lausap lived nearby with Chiwid's younger sister Madeline Palmantier Elkins. Her brother Ollie Nukalow also lived in that area, and her younger brother Scotty Gregg settled near Kleena Kleene.

Chiwid owned several horses over the years and cut hay for them using a butcher knife. At one point she had two or three cows and herded them around to various pothole meadows, feeding them on the small stacks of hay she managed to cut. It was the Grahams of Tatla Lake who nicknamed her the Cattle Queen because of her small herd. Inevitably it was the Grahams or her brother Scotty who ended up feeding her cattle over the winter.

Chiwid travelled widely over the vast Chilcotin Plateau. At first on horseback, leading her string of pack horses, then later on foot, packing everything she owned with her. It was said she'd shoot a moose and would camp right there until she and the ravens and the coyotes had eaten it all up.

Once she got rid of all her horses, Chiwid had a unique manner of shuttling her possessions around the country. She'd start off by carrying one bundle as far as she could while still keeping an eye on her stuff. Then she'd put her load down and go back and fetch another bundle, and repeat the process until she had all her dozen or more bundles in one place. Then she'd start again packing one bundle just as far as she could see.

Chiwid was seen at Farwell Canyon near Riske Creek, over at Big Creek, Nemiah Valley, in the Potato Mountains, around Chilanko Forks, at Siwash Bridge, or fishing through the ice on Anahim Lake.

It was Chiwid's ability to endure the extreme hardships of winter that people marveled at most. With minimum shelter, she would crawl under a tarp in freezing sub-zero weather and still be alive the next day. People speculated on how she was able to do this. Some attributed it to supernatural powers. Others tried to explain it scientifically.

However it was possible, Chiwid was a fixture in the Chilcotin backcountry for more than eighty years, until failing eyesight forced her to finally come indoors for the last years of her life. She stayed with Katie Quilt and Zaloway Setah at Stone Reserve near Hanceville until her death in February 1986.

Several people reached out to her with kindness. In particular Betty Graham Linder of Tatla Lake arranged a small pension for her and would hunt Chiwid down at her various camping spots to bring her food and supplies.

For many people Chiwid embodied the uncanny spirit of independence, self-sufficiency and survival that is characteristic of the Chilcotin. A women's shelter in Williams Lake is named after her, inspiring battered women that anything is possible; that one woman enduring hardships unimaginable, was able to live her life on her own terms.

For a more complete account of Chiwid's life, check out the book, *Chiwid*, published by New Star Books (1995).

Jessie Moon

BY REBECCA ALDOUS

They were childhood sweethearts in the industrial town of Sittingbourne, England, before Charlie Moon left for Canada to seek his fortune in the goldfields of the Cariboo. He was sixteen years old when he came on foot, walking to the Cariboo from Ashcroft in 1888, a distance of about 260 kilometres.

He got only as far as Soda Creek when he changed his mind about going to Barkerville, and crossed the Fraser River to work on a ranch owned by Thomas Meldrum. He decided he'd had enough walking and bought a saddle horse and headed for the Chilcotin.

Charlie decided that land was more valuable than gold and continued to find work on ranches along the west side of the Fraser River. Four years later in 1892, he was employed by Mortimer Drummond at what is now called the Cotton Ranch when twenty-one-year-old Jessie Collard came out from England to be his bride.

The journey was a few weeks crossing the Atlantic, and a week chugging past lakes and the endless prairie on the Canadian Pacific Railway. On November 12, 1892, travel-weary Jessie watched the wheels of her train squeal to a halt in Ashcroft. She stepped off the train into the arms of her fiance, the man she had stayed in touch with through letters for four years. Hours later the two were exchanging vows at the altar.

Jessie Collard before she left England in 1892 is dressed like a lady. When she arrived at Ashcroft in November she had to forego her elegant attire for more practical warmer clothing for the 200-kilometre wagon ride to the Chilcotin.
REX MOON COLLECTION

By mid-November winter was setting in, painting the fields white with hoar frost and snowfall and turning the horses' breath into vapor, like the steam from the train whistle. After four years in the country Charlie had learned how to dress appropriately for the frigid Cariboo Chilcotin temperatures, and brought his new bride a pair of men's felt winter boots to keep her feet warm on the long journey home in the horse-drawn buggy.

Jessie took one look at the ugly oversized boots and right out refused to wear them. However, her dainty high-fashion leather ladies boots she brought with her from London gave her little comfort against the biting cold as they ascended the long incline from the Thompson River valley to the hills of the Cariboo. After a day she relented and exchanged her fashionable footwear for the more practical warmth of felt-lined boots. This incident hinted at the beginning of a different life. Other sacrifices were to follow.

Charlie was a ranch hand on an outfit just south of Riske Creek. He told Jessie that it would take about ten days before she would lay eyes on her new home. With every lift of the horses' hooves Jessie was drawn further away from the society she knew. She had traded the jostle and bustle of the busy port town of Sittingbourne, with its barges piled high with bricks, for adventure in the untamed wilderness of the Cariboo Chilcotin, even though she was deathly fearful of animals.

Eventually Charlie's house came into view. It was a small, one-room log shack, well lived in, with a sod roof. There was no running water nor electricity. The only familiar feature shared by her new home and her house back in England was the outhouse in the back.

Four years later, on July 12, 1896, Jessie gave birth to their first child, a healthy boy, in their humble log cabin. They named him Melville. Meanwhile Jessie had started a vegetable garden to provide food for her budding family. Beyond the propriety of English society, Jessie had learned to become independent and self-reliant. She managed the garden and life in the back country for weeks at a time without her husband present. She wasn't afraid to get her hands dirty or to work up a little sweat on her brow. When it was too wet to hay, she would toil in her garden, picking the weeds between the rows of carrots.

In 1900 when Mel was four years old and able to run around causing normal youngster havoc, Jessie's belly had grown with the anticipation of a second child. On June 2 under a hot summer sky, Jessie, eight months' pregnant, spotted Charlie arriving home on his saddle horse. He had been working all day with the cattle and she swooped Mel into her arms to go meet his father. The family united with waves and smiles and Charlie handed Jessie the reins of his horse while he joyfully picked up his son.

Unfortunately the spirited horse jumped forward, coming down on Jessie's heel. She screamed. The pain was instant and she was unable to walk. The shock caused her to go into labour. Later that night she gave birth to her daughter, Violet, a month premature.

The tiny newborn child was vulnerable as Jessie lay in bed crippled and unable to care for her. At first Charlie placed Violet in the wood stove oven to keep her warm but the worried parents both realized that more was needed. So they turned to the Toosey reserve for help. Two young First Nations women offered to care for Violet, carrying her under their clothing and next to their skin twenty-four hours a day for an entire month. The warmth of their bodies incubated the child, giving her time to grow and get strong. Violet gradually gained colour and put on the weight she needed and finally the care of the two surrogate mothers was no longer required.

Once Jessie could walk again and look after her daughter, she thanked the women for saving Violet's life, but told them she had no money to pay them for their work. Instead she told the women they could take anything of hers they liked. The women looked around the log cabin and each of them took a corset. No other women on the reserve had a corset. This was an item foreign and unobtainable in their community; something exotic. The proud women put on their new attire as if they were sporting new bonnets, and wore their corsets on the outside of their clothes for

"Their corsets were like trophies they wore outside their clothes."

— JESSE MOON

everybody to see. The corsets were their trophies, but more important, they symbolized a bond between the three women and young Violet that lasted a lifetime.

Charlie was still working for Mortimer Drummond in 1901 when he and Jessie decided to go back to England for a holiday. Mel was six and Violet was a year-and-a-half when they made the long journey across Canada by train and then by ship to England so the children could meet their grandparents for the first time. They spent a year in England

Jessie Moon, right, sits on the running board next to her husband Charlie. On the left are their two daughters Dorothy and Violet. Standing behind the car is Fred Becher of Riske Creek. REX MOON COLLECTION

and Charlie started a horse-and-carriage taxi service. One day he met "Young" Davis, a man from the Chilcotin who owned vast tracts of land including Davis Meadow and Deer Park Ranch. Suddenly the Canadian west and open sky tugged at Charlie's heart. Before he knew it, he was shaking the gentleman's hand with agreement to take over control of the land. The total cost was $1,200 with only $40 down for 88 deeded acres at Deer Park and a 200-acre swamp meadow known as the Davis Meadow.

Meanwhile on April 11, 1902, in England, Jessie and Charlie had a new addition to their family with the birth of Rexford Albion Moon, whom they always referred to as Pudge. Later that fall the family made preparations to head back to Canada. This time Jessie had help with the domestic chores as her younger sister Bertha Collard agree to come with the family to look after the children. In November of 1902 the family arrived back in Ashcroft and headed for Deer Park Ranch. Two more children joined the family later, Jack in 1905, and Dorothy in 1909.

As she did before, Jessie kept a garden, planted fruit trees and sold vegetables and fruit to the whole Chilcotin. This enabled Charlie to keep more cattle. In the fall, Jessie would fill up the horse-drawn buggy with boxes of sweet-smelling apples, and she would sell them as far west as Alexis Creek. It would take her two days to get there on the bumpy dirt tracks with her buggy crammed with fresh produce.

Charlie became very successful. Through hard work, frugal living, and thrifty management, he bought up many parcels of land as they became available, until he owned thousands of acres, including the ranch he had first worked on across the river from Soda Creek, owned then by Thomas Meldrum. All three of his sons took after their father, running ranches of their own. Mel ran the Meldrum Creek Ranch, Pudge started at Sheep Creek and later moved to Hill Crest, and Jack took over Deer Park Ranch. As Violet and her sister got to a respectable age they drew many admirers and suitors. However, Charlie was determined to drive them away as soon as they stepped foot on the ranch. He was strict with his daughters, and was going to make quite sure that neither of them married a lowly cowboy. But as fate would have it, Dorothy got married in her mid-twenties to Wes Peterson, whom Charlie did not approve of. Violet took on a different challenge. She had no lack of suitors, and was the first stampede princess for the Williams Lake Stampede. She moved out of her father's house to stay with her brother, Jack, and cooked for him with the same loving dedication as her mother had towards the family. It was not until she was forty years old, which was practically unheard of in her time, before she met a man who gained her heart. But unfortunately not the heart of Charlie.

His name was Tom Sharp and he was from California. He met Violet in the Cariboo and they were instantly attracted to one another. He begged her to return with him to California but Violet would not abandon her brother. Tom returned to California alone, while Violet stayed to help Jack with his ranch. In the winter of 1940, a letter arrived for Tom from Violet. The two had been writing love letters for a while, and with each missive Violet slowly convinced Tom to return to Canada. The letter Tom received on February 4, 1940, was different. Violet wrote of ranches for sale and the goosebumps that covered her skin with thoughts of him. Then she mentioned that Jack was soon to be married. But behind the words this letter had a sombre underlying tone. Tom knew that if he did not head north soon the letters would stop coming. He folded up the letter, and calculated the cost of travelling to Canada on the back of it, then put it in his pocket and made his way to Vancouver.

Charlie did not approve of the relationship between Violet and Tom, even though most of it had been conveyed by pen. Violet had the same adventurous spirit as her mother, and ran away to meet Tom in Vancouver, despite her father's disapproval. Just as hastily as her mother had wed in Ashcroft, she and Tom rushed to the altar. They settled in Quesnel where Tom went into business selling cars and together they farmed potatoes.

Jessie had found freedom in the Chilcotin a world away from the society she grew up in in England. She was self-sufficient with her garden and orchards, and found the space to gain confidence and self-reliance. Like her mother, Violet was strong-willed and spirited. She had beaten the odds at birth, then eventually took a stand and lived her life the way she wanted to.

EDITOR'S NOTE

Information provided by Rex Moon, grandson of Jessie Moon, and his wife Joy Moon. Georgina Moon, Rex's mother, originally told him the story of Jessie and Violet Moon.

Helen Schuk

BY SAGE BIRCHWATER

elen Schuk has a deep appreciation for her life. She almost never got to take her first breath. When her mother, Amelia McGhee, arrived at the small hospital in Alexis Creek on April 16, 1926, after an arduous 160-kilometre journey from Tatlayoko Valley in an iron-wheeled wagon, she was in the midst of a prolonged labour attempting to give birth to her first child. Fortunately the doctor posted in that tiny Chilcotin community knew what to do.

"In those days they didn't do Caesareans," Helen says. "So Dr. Knipthal reached in and found the cord was wrapped around my neck twice. He untangled me and got me out of there." Amelia blamed the long bumpy wagon ride from the lower end of Tatlayoko Valley for causing the birthing difficulty, but Helen's not so sure. She says it could be she was just an active child.

Her parents, Harry and Amelia McGhee, were married in 1923 in Nebraska, and arrived in Tatlayoko in the spring of 1925 in their Model T Ford. They spent a year in Washington state before Harry and his brother Howard journeyed north to look over the Chilcotin. They got as far as Big Creek and liked what they heard about Tatlayoko Valley, so Harry returned to Washington and brought his wife to the new country.

"Newcomers in Tatlayoko Valley always stayed in the Lincoln Creek cabin in those days," says Helen. "Dad bought the place at the head of the lake where Ken Hesch used to stay, and built the first house on that property." Harry cleared the land, sowed crops, and Amelia grew a fabulous vegetable garden. "We had a bit of an orchard there and grew hardy types of fruit," Helen adds.

Helen was sixteen months old when her sister Katie was born in the ranch house next door belonging to K.B. Moore and his wife Dolly on August 15, 1927. She was delivered by Dolly Moore.

"Katie and I would drive the milk cows along behind the wagon."

— HELEN SCHUK

Pioneer life wasn't easy for a woman with two young children, and when Helen was four and Katie was three, Amelia took them to Saskatchewan to visit family. "We left in the fall and took the train to Squamish and the steamship to Vancouver," Helen says. "From there we took the train to Prince Albert, Saskatchewan." Amelia and her two daughters spent all winter on the Canadian prairies before heading south to visit family in Iowa. "Then in the springtime Dad wrote a letter asking Mom to come back, and we returned," Helen says.

When they were old enough for school the McGhee girls were taught by correspondence by Eve Dickinson, who arrived in the country with her sister Joy Graham in the mid-1930s to work for K.B. Moore. When the McGhee girls were growing up, there weren't too many other children living nearby. "Isabel and Beverly Moore were there, but they were quite a bit older than us," Helen says. "Then the Purjues moved in and they had a bunch of kids."

When the Morris Mine opened up on the south end of Tatlayoko Lake, that brought an influx of more people into the valley. As Harry and Amelia got more established, they bought the Charlie Parks place at the foot of the hill coming into Tatlayoko Valley, about fifteen kilometres up the valley from their original ranch. "Dad hayed it for half the hay crop at first," Helen says.

With the luxury of two places at opposite ends of the valley, the family moved with the seasons, summering at the lower place above the lake where Amelia's big garden flourished, and wintering at the Parks Place which produced bumper crops of hay for the animals. "We used to move back and forth at least twice a year," Helen recalls. "Mom had quite a garden there at the lower place. She had a great big patch of potatoes and she sold potatoes." The trouble is nobody had any money to buy anything during the Depression years of the 1930s, so often they had to barter.

There was a barn and a corral at both places. "When it came time for haying we would move down to the Lower Place. We had all the haying equipment at both places except for a rake, which we hauled back and forth in the wagon," Helen says. "We moved the chickens, cats and dogs, and Katie and I would drive the milk cows along behind the wagon. That was our job. We'd make trips back and forth when we needed something."

In the fall the McGhee family would have to roundup their cows off the range in Stikelan Pass or from the Potato Mountains. "Dad would cut out what animals he wanted to sell for beef and he brought those down from the mountain. We would herd what he wanted to sell with Duke Martin's cattle. The drive took nearly a month from Tatlayoko to Williams Lake."

In the meantime Helen and Katie would help their mother harvest the big garden. "We always had a big potato patch, which took all day to dig. We would dig potatoes then we'd load them in the wagon and unload them into the cellar. The turnips and beets didn't take quite so long to harvest. The potato patch was half an acre."

Helen says her dad mostly trapped to make money. "Mostly he went down below Tatlayoko Lake to catch martens and coyotes in the winter. In the springtime there were muskrats."

The first school in the valley was about halfway between the two McGhee properties, where John Kerr lives today. Then it moved up the valley closer to the Parks Place. "I went to school until grade nine, then the war started and there was no more school. Everybody moved out for war-work in the cities."

Helen says the first era of settlers in Tatlayoko Valley in the early 1900s were prospectors. She says the First Nations population got thinned out by smallpox and other diseases like the flu epidemic of 1918, but there was still a small resident native population. "There were the Luluas and Eagle Lake Henry. Eagle Lake Henry was quite notorious. He had the other Indians afraid of him. But he had a big heart. He raised two girls, Mary Jane Dagg, the daughter of Billy Dagg, and Dona Elkins, the daughter of Joe and Matilda Elkins. They gave the Henrys one of their kids. We all went to school together."

"Two sets of sisters married two sets of brothers."
— HELEN SCHUK

Helen remembers the large extended Lulua family who lived between the Chilko River and Tatlayoko Valley. "Old Jack Lulua had Tommy, Eileen and Lashaway in his first family, then Emily, Eliza and Felix in his second family. Katie and I used to play with Tommy's kids, Henry and Jeanie, all the time. They didn't speak much English and we didn't speak any Tsilhqot'in, but we found ways to play just the same."

In the 1940s the two sets of sisters, who grew up together in Tatlayoko Valley, married two sets of brothers. Helen and Katie married brothers, Ed and Joe Schuk, while Mary Jane and Dona married brothers, Pete and Gabby Baptiste.

Helen says the mail used to come into the valley once a month. Then it got to be every two weeks. Del Naomi Haynes was the first postmistress. "Mrs. Haynes had four sons living with her. Ken, her youngest, was only a couple years older than us. Laurie was five or six years older."

Once when she was going to the school halfway up the valley, Helen says she was a bit late getting home one evening. "Dona and Mary Jane walked me up the hill to our fence and Mary Jane gave me a cross she got from the Mission. I suppose it was for protection. Eagle Lake Henry had pulled the girls out of the Mission. He said all they did at the Mission was make them Catholic and he had no use for religion."

Helen Schuk still tends the fires at her home at Cochin Lake near Tatlayoko Valley where she has lived with her husband, Ed, since 1943, and where they raised their seven children. PHOTO SAGE BIRCHWATER

Though Eagle Lake Henry had native ancestry, Helen says he had white rights. This meant he could own deeded land and could legally consume alcohol. The legality of this was challenged one time in the late 1930s when Johnny Blatchford was the Provincial Police officer in Williams Lake, and Eagle Lake Henry was in town all kaiyied for the Stampede. Helen says Johnny caught Henry drinking and started chasing him down the street. "I'm a whikeman! I'm a whikeman!" Henry kept yelling at him.

Helen's mother Amelia went to school for a year to be a nurse before she left Nebraska, and her nursing skills came in handy in the Chilcotin where people were miles away from professional medical care. "Quite often people would come by to get her to do something for them. Sore-Eyed Tommy had glaucoma and Mother would mix up a weak solution of borasic acid and it always made him feel better. Every once in a while he'd come around saying he wanted some of that 'kind of eye medicine.'"

The McGhee ranch at the lower end of the valley was located at the foot of the Potato Mountains, and Helen remembers how wagonload after wagonload of native people would arrive each spring on their way to dig the wild potatoes that grew in the alpine. "Every day several wagons would go by from Redstone or Chezacut. They'd work their way down to the big sidehill at the far end of the mountain range. They had a big camp down at the sidehill where they collected the sap from the Jack pines. Then they'd travel up the mountain as the feed grew for their horses."

She says while the women dug the potatoes, which are about the size of your thumbnail, the men would hunt deer and put up dried meat above a smoky fire. "My dad used to put his cattle up on the Potato Mountains in July. I saw the native women at a distance digging the wild potatoes with a little stick. We weren't allowed to go there."

Helen wasn't quite seventeen years old, and Ed Schuk was twenty-three, when they got married in Williams Lake on February 13, 1943. They had met two or three years earlier at a school picnic at Graveyard Springs near Tatla Lake. "We had sack races and running races and that sort of thing. Then we danced on the grass after that. It was kind of fun." They were the first offspring in either of their families to be married.

Helen and Ed established their place at Lunch Lake on the plateau just north of Tatlayoko Valley, where Charlie Parks once lived. They made their living at first by trapping then gradually got into cattle ranching. Helen and Ed had seven children: Gordon, Alice, Thelma, Doug, Jean, Earl and Lenny. Their family has now expanded to include sixteen grandkids and seventeen great-grandchildren.

When they were ready to retire from ranching, Ed and Helen sold their ranch to their son Earl, with the provision they could spend the rest of their days there, in their house beside the old road between Tatlayoko Valley and Eagle Lake.

"My birthday and Queen Elizabeth's are just five days apart," Helen laughs. "I was born on April 16 and she was born on April 21. So I've always had quite an interest in the royalty."

EDITOR'S NOTE:
This article appeared in *Casual Country*, 2007.

Molly Walker

BY CLINT THOMPSON

Being a child in a modest-income family in Bella Coola would have been very different had we not had Molly Walker in our lives. I am sure that there are people who remember and can historically date Molly's migration to this country and eventually to Bella Coola and I will leave those details to them.

I can't remember meeting Molly as she was already there when I was born in the winter of 1959. Molly adopted my parents when they moved to the "Valley" in the mid-'50s with my two older siblings. Molly became and will always be remembered as a grandma to all of us. She was present on a daily basis and although she must have been very busy just surviving in her own unique way, Molly was always there to give a ride or helping hand to anyone in need.

My brother and I would dig earthworms with Molly in the trees behind her house and she kept them in old galvanized tubs next to her woodshed. She fed them compost and coffee grounds. On summer weekends we would alternately accompany Molly in her Datsun pickup for the 140 kilometres up to Anahim and Nimpo Lakes in the Chilcotin. There she would sell worms by the dozen to the stores and fishing resorts because the cold winters and heavy ground frost prohibited their existence in these areas on a year-round basis.

We would overnight at Harold and Alice Engebretson's, where we were always well fed and had the softest feather beds to sleep in. The next morning, after being properly stuffed with Alice's hotcakes and eggs basted in Rogers Golden Syrup and homemade butter, we would make our way out to Thomas Squinas' where we would back the pickup up to his sheep shed and shovel the box to the brim with sheep manure. This payload was sold as fertilizer to some select gardeners in Bella Coola. I believe the freight companies followed Molly's example and called it the back-haul!

"Molly became and always will be remembered as a grandma to us."

— CLINT THOMPSON

Molly also had fruit trees on her property in Bella Coola and extended her freighting into fall with apples, always returning with the familiar back-haul. Molly could have taught Hodgson Freightways a thing or two about entrepreneurship way back then.

I remember one trip up the "Hill" with Molly when a friend of mine accompanied us. Molly and I always travelled light in the grocery department due to her small appetite and my lack of planning for anything more than one hour in advance. My friend on the other hand had a doting mother who insisted on sending him off with a lunch that would feed the three of us. The mother's inclination for generosity did not transfer through the gene pool to my friend when it came to sharing food, as he immediately started consuming the bag's contents as soon as the truck was set in motion.

Making hay at the Walker place in Atnarko.

It was a very hot summer day and he had eaten most of the food by the time we started up the switchbacks. The combination of the load in the truck, the steep incline, and the heat of the day caused the radiator to overheat and boil over. We were a long way from any help, but a workman from the department of highways happened along in due time and assessed our predicament.

Although we were plenty hot from sitting on that rocky hillside in the hot sun, the Datsun had cooled down to operating temperature and needed about a half-gallon of coolant according to our ministering saviour. The distance to water was too great and he was going in the wrong direction anyway, so the search of both vehicles began. His vehicle came up dry, and ours as well, until in curious desperation the bottomless lunch bag my friend carried was searched and it produced a few cans of soda. These cans were poured into the radiator and topped it up perfectly. This got us to the next water where Molly checked the radiator but it was still full. She and I had a refreshing drink of the cold mountain water but my friend was still so upset about the wasted pop that he refused to drink until he could replenish his loss at the first store in Anahim Lake.

Molly Walker's mother and brother at the Atnarko home in the Bella Coola Valley.

Molly lived alone in an old two-storey house on her acreage in the valley, but was very active in the community. She took photographs and was a correspondent for the *Williams Lake Tribune*. She cut and split her own firewood and hired herself out as a house painter. She was involved with the Valley's Little Theatre Guild, mostly behind the scenes, but also had a role or two on stage.

My father was away from home, working in the logging camps most of the time, and mother didn't drive, so Molly filled in as our driver. Every Thursday was shopping day. In the summer when we were out of school and none of us were old enough or tough enough to fill the role of babysitter, accompanying them became a necessary, if not safer, choice.

There were eventually five of us children and we rode in the box of the Datsun for the twenty dusty kilometres of gravel road from home to the townsite Co-op store and back home again. Frequent stops were made on the return trip as adults visited friends along the way. The Datsun pickup was put to the maximum load test under these conditions, especially on the return trip with the week's groceries in the back.

When the weather was fair, the only inconvenience suffered by us children in the back was the choking dust occasionally stirred up by other motorists, and an occasional insect in the face. However, when the weather turned to rain, the inconvenience shifted to the adults in the cab, where room was now at a premium, not only for five extra bodies but a select bag or two of perishable groceries as well. I have often suspected that some vacationing college students were in the valley one rainy Thursday afternoon and witnessed this spectacle in a passing Volkswagen car. The difference in cubic feet capacity between a 1970 vintage Datsun pickup cab and a Volkswagen Beetle would be interesting to measure in respect to human carrying capacity.

Molly was very resourceful in the ways she chose to make her way through life. I remember other days in the summer months, viewing the world through insect- and mud-filled eyes from the back of the Datsun, while Molly and Mother wound their way up the Valley between the cedar and hemlock trees that towered above the dense alder, cottonwood, and thimbleberry underbrush.

At Firvale, the underbrush disappeared and the forest opened up to mainly Douglas fir of immense size, which dwarfed even the huge off-highway logging trucks we met along the way. The twenty-five kilometres or so from there to the bottom of the hill was covered mostly in this type of forest. We children would play the day away among the giant trees and moss-covered boulders while Mom and Molly worked picking raspberries and blackcaps to put away for our winter's enjoyment.

In her later years, when the property became too large to keep up, Molly sold all but a small piece and moved into a new mobile home set up on the site. She cleaned the brushy lot herself and kept a small garden. Molly was always kept busy clearing and burning the ever-encroaching brush in the corners and edges of her property. The only health problem she had, other than deafness, was the occasional seizure due to epilepsy. Molly sadly passed away one spring day before her time while piling brush in a corner of her property.

It has been said that the impact and influence one makes on his or her fellow man will be reflected in the attendance at their funeral. The church was full of seated and standing friends who all came to pay their respects. Molly was well-loved, sadly missed, and will always be remembered.

Sheila Westwick

BY PAM MAHON

Sheila was born on March 15, 1924, in Manchester, England, the middle child in a family of three, and the only girl. She went to elementary school in Manchester and recalls that having to wear a uniform was a boon to some children; those who could not afford them were supplied with uniforms, but no one else knew that. At eleven, she went on to high school and graduated at age fifteen.

For the next two years, she worked at Kendall Milne Department Store—the Harrods of Manchester. During those years, she became a member of the Weekend Farm Club, as she was too young to join the Land Army. She cycled over to farms every weekend to do volunteer work around Manchester.

In 1941, she signed up with the Land Army. Because so many of the young men working on the farms had joined the Armed Services, young women were recruited to take their places. Sheila was a Land Girl for six years, mainly on mixed farms in South Wales. It was hard work as there was little mechanization—only one farm had a tractor that no one but the farmer's son was allowed to drive. She learned to milk cows, drive the horses, look after chickens, sheep and beef, and every other job on a farm.

One day, when leaving the farm to go home for her twenty-first birthday, she met three men walking along the road. It turned out to be Rudolph Hess, Hitler's aide who had flown a small plane into Scotland the year before, and was in custody in South Wales. He was accompanied by two guards. She remembers him as a tall, striking man with very dark, deep-set eyes.

"Rudolph Hess, Hitler's aide, was a tall striking man, with deep-set eyes."

— SHEILA WESTWICK

Sheila left the Land Army in 1947, and then she enrolled at the Lancashire Agriculture College for a one-year course. In May 1949, she came to Canada with two friends who were sisters. They stayed in Ontario at a farm labour camp for three months, but found the climate very hot and humid. So they took a bus to BC, five days that she will never forget. When they reached Vancouver, one of the sisters got a job in Victoria as a children's nurse; the other went to Mexico to go to art school. Sheila worked in Aldergrove for a Hungarian family who had a berry farm.

After berry season, she went to Keremeos to pick apples, and then finished the season in a cannery in Cawston. She met another girl from Gloucestershire, Bobby, who was trained as a legal secretary. They went back to Vancouver to look for work, but couldn't find any, and didn't really like the city. So early in 1950, they took the train for Prince George. They got off in Williams Lake and booked into the Maple Leaf Hotel.

First impressions of Williams Lake were not positive, but Bobby got a job in Lockwood's lawyers' office and Sheila got one at Lee's Ladies Wear. While there she met Dr. Avery's secretary, Helen, who took her out to Big Lake to meet Irene and Ken McKenzie, who ran the Silverhorn Lodge.

Sheila signed on with them for the season, at a salary of $60 per month. Her duties included milking the cows, wrangling the dude horses, making bread, taking the guests out riding, and any other job that needed doing. When the lodge closed for the season in October, Ken McKenzie went to Kitimat to work as a welder, and Irene moved to a trailer court in Williams Lake with her daughter (who had Down's syndrome). Sheila worked as a dispatcher for the town taxi service and as the agent for the Greyhound Bus. The next April saw her back at the Silverhorn. She recalls that the people living around there at the time made life very interesting. One of the women, Doris Lee, took her flock of sheep up to graze in the alpine meadows every summer.

During the season, Sheila met Freddy Westwick, who had recently returned from Kamloops and was starting a sawmill at Quesnel Lake. This time when the lodge closed in October, she rode her horse from Big Lake over to Bunting Lake, where Freddy was working.

While Freddy was building a log house on the creek, they lived at a logging camp on the YS Ranch near Dragon Lake (which was owned by Fred's parents). Jim was born there in 1953, and they moved to Bunting Lake. They had a sawmill near the lake, and when the senior Westwicks sold the YS Ranch and moved up to the lake, Sheila and Fred pre-empted land to the north, built a house and moved the mill too. They cleared land for pasture and hayfields during the next seven years, and built up a flock of sheep that, at one time, numbered eight hundred. Sheila herded them on Potato Flats, and the Pinette and Therrien field. Edith and Jack Keenan were their nearest neighbours, and it was Edith who taught Sheila how to spin wool.

In 1961, Eric Anderson built a house for Fred, Sheila, and Jim on the shore of Bunting Lake and Jim went to school at 150 Mile. This house burned down in '69, so for five-and-a-half years they lived in a trailer until they could rebuild. During this time, they found that they could not get grazing on the range for their sheep, so they gradually changed over to Hereford cattle. Their first purchase was a bull and seven or eight heifers from Orville Fletcher at 144 Mile House.

Sheila continued working on the ranch and in the mill, and she home-schooled Jim during his high school years. When she turned sixty-five in 1989, Sheila announced her retirement, and concentrated on her many hobbies. She made baskets from spruce roots and willows, knitted toques, socks and sweaters, made comfortable slippers out of strips of stretch material, and even crocheted door-mats from baler twine. Making chairs out of willows and poplar saplings kept her busy for many years. She collected all the material herself and her chairs are now all over BC.

She is a keen gardener though that is now confined to a large greenhouse attached to her home, but her living-room window is filled with exotic plants, most of which she has grown from seed. Mangos were quite a challenge. She is an avid reader, and although she seldom leaves the ranch, Sheila keeps up with all the national and local news. Fred died in 1990, and Jim took over the ranch, sold the mill, and now does some logging. Sheila can be found out walking, knitting or spinning, or making cups of tea for her many friends.

Josephine Gregg

BY SAGE BIRCHWATER

Josephine Gregg has lived most of her life in two worlds, caught between cultures. She was born in the mountains above the Klinaklini Valley in the West Chilcotin in the fall of 1925, but it wasn't until the following spring that her birth was registered by Oblate Priest Father Francois Marie Thomas at the annual Priest Time celebration at Redstone Flats. He listed her official birthday as October 20, 1925, but Josephine says it was likely a month earlier than that.

"It was probably September because my dad, Baptiste Dester, was hunting goats in the mountains. Late October would be pretty late in the year to be up the mountain."

Josephine's mother, Lucy Dagg, gave birth by herself without the aid of a midwife or even her husband. The Tsilhqot'in people were very self-reliant in those days, Josephine says, and it wasn't uncommon for a woman to give birth on her own.

"Living on the land in those days, you got to hunt," she says matter-of-factly.

Priest Time was an annual event that occurred in various aboriginal communities throughout the Chilcotin Plateau and Blackwater drainage when the solitary priest responsible for the region, stationed at the St. Joseph's Mission south of Williams Lake, made a vast circular route that began in Quesnel in the springtime when there was enough green grass to feed his horses. He would head west from Quesnel to Nazko, then continue west to Kluskus, then on to Ulkatcho Village before swinging south following the Dean River upstream to Anahim Lake. From there he would start to circle back towards Williams Lake in an eastward direction to Redstone Flats, then Anaham Flats, Stone and Toosey, eventually making it back home to the Mission in six to eight weeks' time.

Priest Time would be a week-long ordeal in each community holding baptisms, weddings, and blessing the graves of the departed. Instruction in church lore would occur then as well, and the gatherings would be the cause of much celebration featuring lahal games and dancing.

"Father Thomas just guessed my birthday when he baptized me," Josephine says.

Josephine Gregg's two oldest sons, Phillip and Otto, on horseback at Kleena Kleene in the 1950s. Horseback was the only mode of transportation the Gregg family owned for many years.

He also guessed at Josephine's name, which he registered as Seraphine. Later this proved to be a major stumbling block when Josephine and her family attempted to gain their aboriginal status.

Josephine was caught in unusual circumstances, in a no-man's zone between cultures. Her parents both had Tsilhqot'in mothers and absentee white fathers who left their last name for their offspring but not much else. Her mother Lucy Dagg was born to Louisa One-Eye, the daughter of renowned Chief One-Eye. One-Eye Lake near Kleena Kleene is named after him. Her father was George Dagg, a Scotsman, who travelled through the country and sired several children with different aboriginal women across the Chilcotin.

Josephine's father, Baptiste Dester, was born to Yeleucy, a Tsilhqot'in woman from Nemiah Valley. His father was Gerald Dester, a store owner and postmaster at Riske Creek who died in 1902, the year after Baptiste was born.

Because of their mixed ancestry, neither Baptiste nor Lucy had their aboriginal status, and neither did any of their offspring, which included Josephine and her six siblings, Annie, Theresa, Rose, David, Mack and Billy.

Part of the reason for their non-status was intentional. Baptiste chose to relinquish any claim to his aboriginal status so he could own crown land. This meant that his children weren't forced to attend St. Joseph's residential school near Williams Lake like the majority of Tsilhqot'in children growing up in the region.

"I didn't go to the mission residential school in Williams Lake because I had white rights," Josephine says plainly. "My dad let his native rights go so he could buy land." Josephine has mixed feelings about this.

"Maybe we'd have learned something if we had gone," she says, noting that she never really learned to read or write or speak fluent English. "I was glad we never had our status when we were growing up. I didn't want to go to the Mission, even though Father Hennessy tried to help us go there."

Josephine had some schooling, but it was very brief. When she was born her family lived down in the Klinaklini Valley where her father had a trapline. When she was old enough to go to school, her mother moved out to Tatla Lake, about thirty kilometres away, so she and her two older sisters could go to school.

"I went to school for two years at Tatla Lake, in 1931 and 1932. I was doing pretty good but my mother didn't like it there, so we moved to Anahim Lake."

That was the last of Josephine's formal education. She says her father pre-empted some land near Cless Pocket Ranch north of Anahim Lake, then after eleven years, sold it to Billy Dagg, Lucy's half-brother, and moved back down to Kleena Kleene. Her parents separated at that time as well. Eventually Andy Christensen bought Billy Dagg's parcel and added it to his Cless Pocket Ranch, one of the major ranches of the area.

Because of the hard lifestyle trying to make a living in the Chilcotin, Josephine says she never saw her dad very much.

"Dad was always working away some place. We don't see him. In the winter he's trapping way down the Klinaklini Valley past Schilling Lake and we don't see him all winter."

She says in the old days before she was born, her great-grandfather, Chief One-Eye, used to walk all the way to the coast down the Klinaklini Valley. "All he used to take were matches, gun shells and salt."

Josephine spent a lot of time growing up with her grandmother, Louisa One-Eye, around Kleena Kleene. Louisa married an American, George Turner, who many thought was a gunslinger and part of the infamous Dalton outlaw gang. It was speculated that George Turner (an assumed name), had escaped the law south of the border by fleeing to the Chilcotin and Bella Coola Valley. Turner never confided any of these exploits to his family, and as far as Josephine is concerned, they were only rumours.

"Old Turner came from the States and he was a good man. I travelled with my grandmother and Old Turner and their kids, Mary Anne and Young George Turner, around the mountains. Old Turner was good to us. He never got mad at us, not once. I don't think so."

Josephine Gregg and her aunt Maggie Baptiste in the Chilcotin during the 1950s.

But Josephine admits Old Turner was tough. "You can't push him around. If you try it, you'll be on the ground in a little while. One man tried it at Pyper's Stampede at the old Redstone store, and he knocked him out cold. Mistake, I guess."

She says Old Turner had a trapline way down the Kliniklini Valley past her father's trapline. "He'd get lots of beaver, lots of fur. He stayed down there trapping all winter and never came out until May some time. He was a good hunter and a good trapper."

Josephine says it was hard growing up when you had to make a living off the land. "There was no welfare. In the olden days before I remember, Grandma and Old Turner would go to the store at Hanceville (more than 160 kilometres east of Kleena Kleene) driving a team and wagon. They would camp along the way."

Josephine says one reason she knows a lot of old-fashioned stories is because she stayed with her grandmother so much. "I never learned to read or write so maybe that's why I could remember these stories so well. I used my own language [Tsilhqot'in]. It's pretty hard to keep it [the old stories and history] when you're speaking English all the time."

She says she eventually learned to speak English from her own children when they started attending school many years later. "I learned quite a bit [of English] when the kids come home from school. They teach me quite a bit."

Once Babtiste sold out his place at Cless Pocket and he and Lucy split up, Josephine says she and her siblings scattered all over the country.

Josephine grew up in Anahim Lake with her future husband Scotty Gregg, but they lost touch with each other briefly when she moved away to Kleena Kleene after her parents separated.

"I went away for one or two years to stay with my dad at Kleena Kleene, then I came back to Anahim Lake again."

She says she and Scotty got married at the Anahim Lake schoolhouse during Priest Time, on June 21, 1948.

"I learned to tan my own hides when I was eleven years old."

— JOSEPHINE GREGG

"Everybody was mad at us because I steal somebody's boyfriend. There was no church. Everybody lined up and got married. The next day Andy and Annie Cahoose got married."

Josephine and Scotty made their home at Porcupine Meadow near Kleena Kleene, and together they had seven children: Elsie, Otto, Phillip, Jack, Garry, Judy and Joanne.

"We used horses for a team to cut hay and pull a wagon. We moved around in the summertime for jobs, then back to Kleena Kleene so the kids could go to school in Tatla Lake. They stayed in the dorm at Tatla Lake."

Josephine says Scotty worked on various ranches around the country, guiding and training horses.

"He was breaking horses all the time and worked at Cless Pocket a long time too, and worked for Fred Engebretson at Towdystan. I mostly stayed at Kleena Kleene with the kids. Scotty was away so much working, the kids didn't know their dad."

She says they usually got their food at Ike Sing's store in Anahim Lake, about sixty kilometres away.

"It was pretty hard to go to the store. The mail truck would go up once a week, and I'd catch a ride when we needed some groceries. I'd have a babysitter stay with the kids."

Joanne Butler, Josephine's youngest daughter, says there was no electricity or running water when they were growing up.

"I remember Mom washing the clothes by hand. We went to school in Kleena Kleene. I had Mrs. Krause and Mrs. O'Fee for our teachers."

Josephine was well-known for her buttery-soft buckskin which she tanned and sewed into moccasins and gloves and other articles of clothing. "I learned to tan my own hides when I was eleven years old. I helped my grandma and my mom."

She says her buckskin has gone all over the world. "My moccasins and gloves go to Germany and Mexico."

When she moved to Kleena Kleene as a teenager to look after her dad's cows for two years, Josephine says she would spend the summer tanning about fifteen deer hides, then sewed buckskin all winter. In those days she said she never had beads or coloured embroidery thread to decorate her buckskin. Instead she did appliqué work by sewing coloured material on the back side of the buckskin and cutting and sewing the hide to reveal the colourful patterns. Joanne says her mother sewed all the clothes for her children when they were small.

While Josephine has retired from the physically demanding work of tanning deer and moose hides these days, she continues to sew and bead gloves and moccasins when she can get some buckskin. One of her pastimes is to sew miniature items from commercial hide as souvenirs. "My family buys it off of me and hangs it in their windshield."

One of the biggest challenges Josephine and her family encountered was trying to obtain their First Nations status. Joanne, who did much of the legwork, says it took thirteen years to work their way through the bureaucracy of the federal government and the Catholic Church. One of the problems was that Josephine couldn't read or write. Once they realized that she was registered as Seraphine on the baptismal records of the Church, things went a lot smoother. They still had to prove that they were First Nations even though Josephine's first language was Tsilhqot'in. "Baptiste's grandfather was Chief Nemiah," says Joanne.

Josephine's husband, Scotty Gregg, had a similar plight with his status. His Tsilhqot'in mother, Lausap, was deaf and mute, and his father was a wandering Scotsman by the name of Frank Gregg. "Dad didn't have a last name on his baptismal record," Joanne says, noting that they finally got help from Tsilhqot'in elders Donald Ekks and Emily Lulua. "They told the lawyer that Lucy's mom was full Indian."

In later life Josephine adopted Joanne's first-born son, Skipp Gregg, and raised him as her own child. Besides her seven children, in 2009 she had fifteen grandchildren and fifteen great-grandchildren.

EDITOR'S NOTE
This article appeared in *Casual Country*, 2009.

Coming Later

NEW PERSPECTIVES AND SKILLS

Dinah Belleau in her pow wow dancing regalia.
Right: Dinah Belleau with fellow gardeners Doreen Ann Johnson and Mary Daniels in the
Esket garden at Alkali Lake. PHOTOS LIZ TWAN

Dinah Belleau

BY LIZ TWAN

Dinah Belleau grows food for her people to eat. She has a love for gardening and a talent for making her produce grow bigger and better than most—her thumb is greener than green. She is the head gardener at the Esketemc First Nation reserve at Alkali Lake—she works under the umbrella of Esketemc Agriculture and she guides two assistants in the art of vegetable production.

Dinah was born on December 12, 1943, and raised at Esket, a place she has come and gone from quite a few times over the past years. But, one of her longest stints away from home began in 1977 when she spent twenty years off and on living with the CEEDS group in Miocene, east of Williams Lake, and at Horse Lake near 100 Mile House. CEEDS is an acronym for the Community Enhancement and Economic Development Society. The people who make up CEEDS believe in being able to supply all of their own needs to be self-sufficient. To that end they raise their own meat: beef, pork, lamb, chickens, etc. (all natural) and raise their own produce—all organic.

Dinah "the garden lady" learned her gardening expertise during her time with CEEDS, where she also spent two summers herding sheep in the mountains near Crooked Lake, using a motor bike and dogs to move the flock. In the late 1990s Dinah came back to Esket (for good it appears this time) and brought with her all the knowledge learned over years through helping to grow massive gardens with CEEDS at various sites in the Cariboo and Chilcotin. "I felt guilty being away so long," she says. "All the elders and my friends were passing away, and I wanted to live with my own people. I'm thankful for the years I spent with CEEDS."

"You're supposed to talk to your plants."

— DINAH BELLEAU

For the garden at Esket, Dinah begins with the best. She orders her seed from the William Dam company—purveyors of very fine untreated seed. She tries to vary what they order and gets new types of vegetables each year (on a limited basis). Some things grow better than others in the area. The women learn what varieties do best, through trial and error. The Esket garden team keeps a garden journal (record book) with the varieties planted and other useful garden tips and information for reference the following year.

Dinah says, "I don't think the people here like the colour purple. Every purple thing I've ever grown in this garden has been hard to give away. I grew purple beans last year (they turn green when cooked) and no one wanted to eat them!"

The produce they grow is delivered by the boxful to families on social assistance to help provide nutritious choices for people on a limited budget. The elders also receive vegetables and the Elder's Tuesday luncheons often feature soup or stew made with community garden veggies. The children from Daycare and the Headstart program are regular visitors to the garden—they come for walks and check the garden's progress. The garden plot is huge and Dinah and her assistants work hard to plant, water, weed and harvest. Dinah is a happy good-natured woman who is training her helpers Doreen Ann Johnson and Mary Daniels to take over from her once she retires. "I told them I'm going to retire. This is my last year." I'm not sure that I believe her, she loves the garden. She winks and admits that she might "come by from time to time to see how they're doing."

Mary Daniels is a tiny, hard-working woman; she probably doesn't even make the scale hit the one-hundred-pound mark. She hails from Canim Lake originally, but now calls Alkali Lake home—a working mother, she has one son, Roland Dick. Mary worked previously as a homemaker and at the daycare centre—this is her second year in the garden with Dinah. She says that when she took the job last year it was because it was the only job available, but the garden work has grown on her and she really enjoys what she does now. The ladies work from 8:30 a.m. to 4:30 p.m. the five weekdays and they take a rest on weekends. Mary is responsible for the journal records of the garden, a task she began last year.

The other garden assistant, Doreen Ann Johnson, looks at her thumb and announces that it still looks brown. She has only about a week of experience to this point. Last year Doreen put in a few hours here and there helping out. She is also small in stature and the mother of a grown-up son, Jonathon Hutchinson, and two teenage daughters, Dawn and Ann Marie. She might be the garden's rookie, but she is not a youngster. Doreen has previously worked as a homemaker and in the janitorial field.

Dinah says, to me, "The girls will spend the summer keeping the garden weed-free." Then she laughs heartily and says that there were probably only one or two weeds that she could spot last year.

There are a few other large garden plots in progress; they belong to Marge Dick, the Chelsea family, the Johnson family, and others. The grow-your-own bug is catching on with Alkali Lake's Esketemc First Nation Band. Veggies, that is!

ↄↄ

AUTHOR'S NOTE

It turned out that I was correct when I said that I doubted that Dinah would retire. The 2008 garden season has come and gone with Dinah at the helm of the "garden ship." She planted an even bigger garden with a larger crew under her command. Felix Robbins, Dale Johnson, April Robbins, Mary Daniels, Mallory Paul and Donna Robbins were some of Dinah's assistants this season. As I write this postscript they are harvesting the garden. Five hundred pounds of potatoes and three hundred pounds of carrots are going to the Sxoxomic School for their in-school lunch program. Other customers include the Elders' program and the Alkali Lake Ranch bunkhouse as well as individual purchasers, who are happy to purchase high-quality organic produce.

Recipe for Deer Stew

According to Dinah, the key to making a good stew or soup is the availability of plenty of fresh, organic vegetables. She has an abundance at her garden in Esket Village. Dinah says when you have a large garden like she does, the only way to use up the veggies is to make lots of stews. She says one secret to growing a good garden is to talk to it. "You're supposed to talk to your plants."

INGREDIENTS

Potatoes, carrots, turnips, onions, garlic, broccoli, cauliflower, green pepper, peas, beans, zucchini squash, chard, and other vegetables, deer meat cut up in bite-sized chunks, salt and seasoning to taste.

PREPARATION

Brown the deer meat in a large cast iron pot or frying pan with a small amount of oil or lard. As the meat is browning add chopped onion and garlic. Put water, potatoes, carrots and turnip into a large pot and bring to a boil. Add the browned deer meat, onion and garlic. Once the potatoes, carrots and turnip have softened somewhat, add the other vegetables. If you want more broth, add more deer meat.

EDITOR'S NOTE

There were no funds to hire a crew to put in a community garden in the spring of 2009. Finally Dinah and her friend Mary Daniels got busy in early July to plant about an acre of potatoes and other vegetables. The seeds had been ordered and Dinah couldn't stand the thought of them going to waste. So she and Mary got busy. They arranged to have the garden plot rototilled up, then they weeded and planted it. Gardening is in both women's blood now. Dinah's green thumb won't let her rest. The concept of retirement takes second fiddle to her passion to work on the land. "As long as my bones can take it," she says. "So far it's okay."

This article appeared in *Casual Country*, 2007.

Win Bennie

BY SAGE BIRCHWATER

Win Bennie lived in the same house in downtown Williams Lake for more than fifty years. She and her husband, Fred, and two of their three kids moved into the house in the early 1950s. Their third child, Sally, was born in Williams Lake a few years later.

Win's house is perched on top of the knoll overlooking the city and the Stampede grounds, and from that vantage point she watched the city grow up around her. She saw it shake off its sleepy cow town image and transform into a bustling sawmilling town and government service centre. Win preferred things more slowed down and natural, and was one of the town's first naturalists and an environmentalist. "If you love the outdoors and the creatures in it, you have to be concerned about their well-being," she always said.

Win came by her love of nature honestly. "I spent my childhood on the Stuart River, about two miles this side of Fort St. James. We had a farm with a couple of milk cows and three horses and a bunch of chickens and geese. You could see sturgeon coming to the banks of the river when the ice went out. I was always an outdoor child. My mother put me in coveralls."

Back in the 1950s things were pretty natural around Williams Lake. Win's oldest daughter Barrie had a horse she kept in the barns at the Stampede grounds. "That horse spent a good bit of time up here at the house," Win laughed.

In those days she said her daughter made enough money babysitting to pay for all the expenses for keeping her horse. "The roads were dirt and some streets had wooden sidewalks. Our youngest daughter learned to ride a horse before she could walk."

It was during the 1950s that the environmental movement first got underway in Williams Lake. Elton Anderson of the Federation of BC Naturalists encouraged a small group of people in the community to establish a local branch of the FBCN organization in the Cariboo. "We had many meetings in our house. Elton was very persistent," Win recalled. "He felt it was important to have a group in the Cariboo."

"People need to slow down... and look at the natural world."

— WIN BENNIE

Through Anderson's support, the Williams Lake Field Naturalists group was formed. A short time later the group helped establish Scout Island Nature Centre, an environmental jewel in the province's Interior. "There was a strong movement to develop Scout Island for industry and to fill in the marsh," Win recalled. "About twelve or fifteen of us wrote letters. They didn't develop it. Someone listened to those letters instead."

Today Scout Island Nature Centre is one of the best known birding habitats adjacent to urban development in the province. Win said a lot of credit goes to former mayor Tom Mason. "We were very lucky to have Tom Mason for mayor. He was all for Scout Island. If he hadn't said the Field Naturalists should take on the Nature Centre, it would have gone commercial."

Once Fred Bennie retired from his job as city parks manager and foreman of the ice arena, he and Win spent a lot of time outdoors keeping track of the birds across the Cariboo Chilcotin. "We did a breeding bird survey. We started at 4:00 in the morning and used to go with our dog and two cats and sleep in the canopy of our truck. We met so many people in the naturalist group."

Fred and Win also had a cabin on Nimpo Lake where they went to "get away from it all." Now it belongs to the Nature Trust of BC. "The cabin was a place of healing for me," Win recalled. "We did nesting and loon surveys at Nimpo." She said one time her oldest grandson, Shane, who was thirteen at the time, returned home from an intensive six-week figure skating school in North Vancouver. "He walked over to our house with his little dog and said, 'Gramma, can we go to Nimpo?' All he wanted to do was be out there in the quiet. He didn't want to be organized. He just wanted to be. He never continued with his skating after that."

Three hip replacements allowed Win to stay active for several years after Fred passed away. She got her exercise by walking her dog Missy and two cats, Puss and Muffin. "I'm not lonely and I'm not bored with my animals," she would say.

Though she had a bird feeder on her porch, Win and her pets worked out a system where everybody got along. When she went outside with Missy for an hour or two each day, she let her two Siamese cats outside as well. "I put covers over the bird feeder to protect the birds from the cats." Her cats rarely caught any birds. "When they did the birds often got away."

Members of the Field Naturalist group were like a large extended family for Win. "Usually things work out for the better if you just wait," she would say philosophically. "The Lord is good. Of course I don't move around very fast any more, but members of the Field Naturalists and the United Church bring the news to me about the places in nature I can't get to any more." And her friends from this close-knit group were always there to help her. Somebody always took Missy for her walks and picked Win up to go out or go shopping. One member of the group even planted her garden.

Toward the end of her life Win was asked what advice she had for the younger generation. "People need to slow down and take time to look at the natural world," she said. "Take time to observe what's around us, and observe what is natural." The old slogan: "To know Nature and keep it worth knowing," was one of her favourite sayings.

EDITOR'S NOTE:
This article appeared in *Casual Country*, 2005.

Maree Benoit

Before my husband and I moved to Williams Lake in 1963, I had been involved in the Mayfield Community Playschool in Edmonton. At that time there was only one training program for playschool and preschool instructors at the University of Alberta. My neighbours encouraged me to take this six-week course. I took their advice, and so when I arrived in Williams Lake I had a basic background in children's activities.

My local career in childcare started at Cynthia Mason's playschool called Puss and Boots, here in Williams Lake, where we took our son Moray and volunteered from time to time. When the Skyline School moved to its present location and became Kwaleen School, Mrs. Armes asked me to do a grade one preparation class for the children going into the new school. This eventually led to a preschool program and then a kindergarten.

Our family moved out to Meldrum Creek for a couple of years and while we were there a daycare society was formed and the daycare was built on its present site. It was quickly filled up with twenty-five children, then the board decided to finish the downstairs and enroll another twenty-five children. I was hired to cook and clean and to act as a general daycare worker. There was a growing need for space for special needs children.

Maree Benoit and her preschool group enjoy a group activity in Boitanio Park in Williams Lake.

BC Rail Land became available next to the daycare, so a committee was formed to build the present Child Development Centre. Today it is considered one of the most up-to-date and successful centres in BC.

In 1974 there was a growing need for certified preschool teachers, so a group of us approached Cariboo College to request that a training program be started. Four years later, four of us were certified: Marlene Hanson, Gerry Withler, Margaret MacDonagh, and myself. Muriel Garland of Williams Lake asked me to take over a playschool group that was having trouble getting started in the basement of the Anglican Church. Our little group grew, and after two years we moved into the Sacred Heart hall.

There was a big demand for pre-schools at this time, and Jean Wellburn set up a program at Scout Island Nature Centre. This preschool experience is still in demand because of the nature studies. In 1979, and I became interested in starting my own home daycare, and on January 1, 1980, Mary Poppins Day Care opened next to Crescent Heights School. This was the first licenced home daycare in Williams Lake for ten children.

"I made it my goal to make sure that all children have the very best care..."

— MAREE BENOIT

One summer the Child Development Centre wanted an English as a Second Language (ESL) program for new Canadians moving to Williams Lake. The Sikh community and School District 27 sponsored the program for twenty children, and the school board incorporated this program into the primary schools.

Maree Beniot engages children in activities at the Williams Lake and District Day Care Centre.

The administrator of Sugar Cane approached me about setting up a daycare for the children on the reserve that would follow the theme of their native cultural heritage. I contracted this for one year until two women from the Sugar Cane community received early childhood education training.

The Women's Contact Centre has been instrumental in raising the quality of care for small children. A good example is the Kid Care Daycare program up at Columneetza Secondary for students continuing their education. This allows the women to have contact with their babies during the day, which is very important to allow the bonding to happen that is crucial in the first year of life.

Because children learn most of their cognitive skills before the age of six, I made it my goal to make sure that all children have the very best of care in their early childhood years. Now all licencees are required to have their training, police checks, and first aid courses up to date, and their centres must be up to regulation standards. I'm happy to say that Williams Lake has wonderful preschools and daycares. The school district is also getting involved in showing parents how they can take an active part in preparing their children for kindergarten. The progress that has happened in the last forty years is momentous, but it takes societies like the Women's Contact Centre and the Child Development Centre to keep the advancements coming.

Velma McDermott Derrick

BY GLORIA ATAMANENKO

Velma McDermott Derrick was raised in the Boisie Valley of southeastern Oregon. She was the eighth of twelve children. Five siblings of this large family still remain and hold reunions nearly every year. Theirs was a hard-working farm family, with a mother who taught love and courtesy, and a father who played the violin to his family every evening.

In her teens, Velma met a rancher's son, Elmer (Tuffy) Derrick. Tuffy grew up with horses and knew how to handle them and break them to the saddle. He soon taught Velma to ride horseback, and the farm girl's interest changed to ranching. It was wartime, Tuffy was drafted, and he and Velma were in love and wanted to get married. There was no time to plan a big, traditional church wedding. Eighteen-year-old Velma left the college she was attending, and she and Tuffy travelled to nearby Reno, in neighbouring Nevada, and were married in a civil ceremony there. Fifty years later, they travelled back to Reno, repeated their wedding vows in a chapel, and returned home to 150 Mile House. Daughter Beverly hosted a lovely reception for them at Miocene Hall.

The Derricks came to 150 Mile House in 1955 when Tuffy was offered a job by rancher Huston Dunaway. It was a cold, snowy winter, much harsher than the milder, drier climate of eastern Oregon. One night they left the tap in the sink running so that

Velma Derrick reads a card while opening gifts at a family celebration.

the water pipes would not freeze. In the morning, there was a cone of ice in the sink: "Niagara Falls!" joked Tuffy.

The cold weather in the Cariboo was balanced by the warm friendliness and generosity of the people. Nearest neighbour, Sherry Overton, visited Velma and became a lifelong friend. Other neighbours also welcomed the young American couple and their two little girls. For Velma, who was very shy at that time, their friendliness felt wonderful.

Velma noticed that the curriculum and other aspects of the local school were very different from the elementary school in Oregon. She decided to join the Parent Teacher Association so that she could learn more about the Canadian school system. In time, she was elected secretary of the PTA.

In 1958, Tuffy took the job as manager of the Williams Lake Branch of the BC Livestock Producers Co-operative Association, a position he held until his retirement twenty-nine years later. Honest, straightforward, ever-helpful, Tuffy Derrick was greatly respected and appreciated by the ranchers for whom he worked.

The manager's job was very demanding of Tuffy's time. Velma, who had never worked outside the home, wanted to work at Tuffy's workplace, "so that I could meet the people he worked for and understand better what he did. Then I would know better how to talk with him when he got home." When the ages of their two little Canadian-born sons allowed it, and a position at the Co-op became available, Velma went to work there also. She was employed there for twenty-one years.

Velma's original motivation to take the job was simply to share more fully in Tuffy's life, but she soon found that the work was deeply satisfying for its own sake. It was a complex, fast-moving job and Velma learned to do every aspect of it. On sale days, the breeds, ages, colours, weights, and sex of the animals had to be recorded, as well as the names of their owners. Each animal had to be weighted before being auctioned, and the old weight scale, used for many years, meant a lot of exacting work. At the end of the day, there was a mass of information to record and balance.

As the years went on, Velma, who knew every aspect of the work involved, became personnel manager of the eight to ten people who worked at the Co-op. She tried to be very careful in hiring workers, choosing well-motivated people who would be congenial with one another. She taught them their various jobs and spelled them off when they needed breaks.

On the mornings after every sale day, Velma prepared the cattle market report for the BC Livestock Association of Williams Lake and read it on the local radio station. She loved doing that and was commended many times for her performance. The ranching families appreciated hearing the report and thanked Velma for doing it.

When changing times brought computers, Velma astonished people by finding these new contraptions exciting rather than formidable! She learned to use them quickly. Just another challenge to meet and overcome!

> *"The cold weather in the Cariboo was balanced by the warm friendliness of the people..."*
>
> — VELMA DERRICK

In 1974, Tuffy and Velma fulfilled a lifelong dream and bought a ranch of their own. They, their children Beverly, Deanna, Clifford, Randy, and their families, enjoyed it greatly for twenty years.

Once again, Velma worked with Tuffy, becoming his right-hand helper. Building and repairing fences, they walked the perimeters of the whole ranch. Velma learned to pull calves when cows had difficult births, and she helped with branding. Sometimes she had to search for heifers that hid themselves in outlying corners of the ranch to deliver their calves. In wintertime, she climbed to the tops of hay-bale stacks to scrape off the snow so that the bales could be brought down to feed the cattle. She was a hard-working and deeply appreciated helpmate.

When Tuffy's health made it too difficult to work and live on the ranch, the Derricks sold it to friends and moved to Okanagan Falls. The climate is so much warmer there, and there is still some ranching activity, but Velma traded her horse for a bicycle! She swims and cycles, is an active member of the Women's Institute, and plays cribbage at the seniors' centre. Her children visit her and she visits them frequently, in the Cariboo. "And," she says, "I am happy!"

Diana French

BY GAEIL FARRAR

When Diana French was attending Normal School in Victoria to become a teacher she never dreamed her career choice would take her to the remote Chilcotin, where she would begin her evolution into a consummate historian, journalist, book author, columnist, political activist, school trustee, and last but certainly not least, the loving matriarch of a large, extended family, some of whom have been unofficially adopted into the French family over the years.

The road ran north and the pavement stopped at Lac la Hache that fall day in 1951 when Diana Endersby arrived in the remote Chilcotin community of Chezacut to start her first teaching position. Diana's father, Frank, and brother, Don, drove her to Chezacut, taking two days to make the trip from their home on Quadra Island to Williams Lake.

There was a cattle sale in progress and the only available accommodation in the lakecity was a tent with a wooden floor and sides that sat behind a motel. "There wasn't any heat and it was cold," remembers Diana. They headed west the next day.

They had instructions to go to Randolph Mulvahill's ranch at Chezacut. Their A-7 Austin wasn't built for dirt roads. "It was like riding in the inside of a vacuum cleaner bag. That was the first of many dusty rides," she exclaims.

Randolph's wife Goldie had a large hay crew and six children to feed but she didn't bat an eye when three strangers arrived on her doorstep. Ever gracious, she fed them, "and even found beds for us," Diana says. When her father saw that the actual teacherage his nineteen-year-old daughter would be living in was several miles from any other habitation, he wanted to take her back home again.

The one-room teacherage sat on blocks. It had an outhouse, a well with a wonky pump, a wood stove for cooking and heating, a woodpile and an axe, and a gas lamp for light, remembers Diana. Born in Campbell River, and raised on Quadra Island, she was no stranger to rural life, but she had never lived in a house without indoor plumbing or electricity. This accommodation was not her idea of a good time.

Diana and Bob French at their wedding in July 1952 at Campbell River. They said their vows in the Campbell River Hospital Chapel.

She had been a somewhat sheltered teen, attending St. Ann's Academy in Victoria for high school and Normal School and then the University of BC in Vancouver. Chezacut was comprised of three ranches and a store. Only one ranch was beyond the teacherage, and that family came by once a week for the mail, Diana says. The school, which had opened the year before, had sixteen children in grades one to six, but textbooks for grades five and six didn't arrive until the end of October. "That was a challenge."

The Chezacut school was independently run at the time and had its own school board, which consisted of the storekeeper and two of the three ranchers who were in charge of ordering supplies, maintenance, and whatever else needed doing. The children rode saddle horses to school, although one family came by cutter in winter. That first year Diana didn't have a vehicle or a horse. Most of her travelling was done "doubling" or riding behind with the student who had the gentlest horse. "And hanging on for dear life."

Diana says she only learned to ride out of necessity. The water in the well at the teacherage was too hard and scummy to drink so the students brought drinking water from home for themselves and for her. They brought the water in used whiskey bottles tied to their saddles. "The rows of whiskey bottles at the back of the classroom startled the school inspector," Diana smiles.

The students also became the teachers in other ways. "I was afraid to light the gas lamp myself so one of the older kids would light it before they went home," says Diana.

She took the job in Chezacut because it came with isolation pay which was almost twice that of teaching jobs in other communities. She planned to teach for two years then use her earnings to return to university. But fate had another plan—one that would start a lifelong adventure and love affair with the Cariboo Chilcotin, its history, its people, and a certain man.

Born at Kleena Kleene, and raised at Riske Creek and Alexis Creek, Bob French was cowboying for his sister, Mary, and brother-in-law, Ollie Knoll, at the Chezacut Ranch when he came to the teacherage one frosty September day to fix the well's broken pump. Bob and Diana quickly became acquainted and were married the next summer (1952). They celebrated their fiftieth wedding anniversary in 2002. They had just three weeks between the end of branding season at the end of June and the beginning of haying season at the end of July to get married and squeeze in a two-week honeymoon. They borrowed Diana's brother's car for their honeymoon, but forgot to take a letter of permission with them for the car when they crossed the border into the US. All they had was their personal identification and their word.

The border crossing guard told Bob that anyone who was born at Kleena Kleene and lives at Chezacut and is driving a car registered at Quathiaski Cove on Quadra Island couldn't possibly be making it up.

Diana taught at Chezacut for two years after they were married. They lived at Chezacut Ranch and when the roads permitted, Diana drove Bob's pickup to school, collecting five students along the way. The older ones rode in the back. She didn't have a driver's licence for the first school year because she was never in Williams Lake on a weekday to get one. When she did finally write the test in Williams Lake she was told to take the road test in Alexis Creek.

"Bob Turnbull, the police officer there at the time, told me not to bother with it because he knew I'd been driving all the time."

In 1975 Ollie bought a Gallion grader and rented it out to the Highways department. Bob went with it, snowplowing the Chilcotin Road between Alexis Creek and Anahim Lake in winter and grading in summer. When Highways bought a new grader in 1957, Bob left the ranch, and began a thirty-three-year career on the road crew working for the government. The French family moved to Alexis Creek that summer. For a short time they lived in the old one-room school that Bob had attended as a kid.

The grader was accompanied by a swamper with a truck and a small travel trailer. The swamper carried supplies, picked rocks off the road, cleared out ditches and culverts and did the cooking. In the summer Diana and the kids went along.

"We packed up the kids, the cat, the dog and went with him," Diana says.

As long as Diana was doing the cooking the swamper didn't mind sleeping in the French's delivery sedan while the family slept in a trailer that was always parked close to the road. The travellers often stopped for a visit, a coffee, or a meal, and Diana met a lot of people. Her favourite swamper was the late Willie Johnson, who was also a guide outfitter in the Chilcotin country. "He had a big box with everything in it. No matter what I needed, he had it, from tweezers to an emergency first aid kit," says Diana. "Whenever we went visiting in the van, we had to be home in time for him to go to bed. He was pretty special. He would tell the kids stories and find wild strawberry patches for them."

"That trailer got smaller when it rained."

— DIANA FRENCH

They moved camp every three or four days. Sometimes they would stay in the emergency cabins established along the highway. Once, while they were staying in one of them, Diana managed to fill the small wood-fired oven with one loaf of homemade bread. She's not sure what she did wrong or right but it was still edible after being pried out of the oven. "The crust was really nice and crunchy."

Bob's schedule was on the road ten days and home for four days. In spite of being away most of the summer they grew a huge garden. The family continued to camp out in summers with Bob until there were four boys under the age of seven. "That trailer got smaller when it rained," says Diana.

One evening when Diana had diapers hanging out on a line, strung between the trailer and the grader, they received a visit from MLA Bill Speare who had come up for the Anahim Lake Stampede. "He was a bit taken aback by the laundry but he thought it was a great idea for the family to be there," says Diana.

In 1962, the French family moved to Anahim Lake where the Highways maintenance yard had just opened. Bob was the third foreman to tackle the job in ten months. The first two hires buckled under the stress of trying to keep the Bella Coola Road open in winter. Fairly regularly, Bob was pulling people out of a snowbank or ditch and getting them going again. "But I don't think anyone ever got into serious trouble," says the laconic Bob.

In winter the boys skated on the Chilcotin/Bella Coola Highway. The road was often closed because of ice and snow conditions and the "highway" by the house would be solid ice, Diana says.

Diana returned home to Quadra Island to give birth to their two oldest sons, John and Mike, who were born in the hospital at Campbell River on Vancouver Island. Bob and Diana had been married in that hospital chapel. Son Paul was born in the old Williams Lake hospital, where City Hall is now, and son Bill was born in the Red Cross Hospital at Alexis Creek. "Bill and Bob belong to a select group. They were both actually born in the Chilcotin," Diana says. A fifth son, Mark, was born in the Bella Coola Hospital, while the family was living in Anahim Lake.

With five children in tow, Bob and Diana moved to Bridge Lake in the South Cariboo in 1965, where Bob worked as the Highways road foreman for five years. "Winters were colder then. The house at Bridge Lake was on a hill and at forty below, moose would sun themselves on the slope in front of the house."

While raising the children Diana also did some teaching. She and Edna Telford shared teaching grades one to six at Alexis Creek for a year. "It was a unique team teaching arrangement. Edna taught in the morning while I looked after her two little ones, and I taught in the afternoon while she looked after my two." Diana also substitute taught at Anahim Lake and Bridge Lake. She started writing for magazines while living in Anahim Lake and was a rural correspondent for the *Williams Lake Tribune* while they were living in Bridge Lake.

Government housing was provided for the family at both Anahim Lake and Bridge Lake but neither house was ready when they arrived so they ended up living in a travel trailer for several months until the houses were ready. "The first house at Bridge Lake was tiny and mice, rats and a skunk took up residence under the house." Bridge Lake only had an elementary school and Bob and Diana couldn't see sending their kids to live at the dorm in 100 Mile House for school, so in 1970 Bob transferred to the Highways department in Williams Lake, and Diana substitute taught almost full-time that year.

Ever the political activist, her first battle after arriving in Williams Lake came in 1971 when she joined a community group that was protesting a plan by the municipality to pump raw sewage into the Fraser River. "I went snorting in to publisher Clive Stangoe because I thought the paper was neglecting city council news. He responded by hiring me and I got stuck covering city meetings," says Diana. "I didn't know how to type. Actually I still don't. My copy was always messy." But that didn't stop her from becoming a full-time staff reporter for thirteen years, the last five as editor. The *Tribune* won national and provincial awards when she was editor and she also won a provincial award for her editorials.

Through their sons' teen years during the 1970s the Frenchs' home became an open house for all their kids' friends. Some would just move in for a time before getting things sorted out at home. They never knew who was going to be coming upstairs for breakfast but Bob never complained and they never had cause to chase any of the kids out.

"We must be related to the Pied Piper because we can't remember when we haven't been knee-deep in children," says Diana.

Raising five boys and a foster son who all played hockey, Bob and Diana practically lived at the arena and she served on the minor hockey executive for years. When Diana was working, she and Bob had an arrangement that whoever came home first started dinner. Diana left the *Tribune* in 1984 and returned as a columnist in 1995.

Since retiring she has had two books published by Harbour Publishing: *The Road Runs West: A Century Along the Bella Coola/Chilcotin Road*, and *Ranchland: British Columbia's Cattle Country* with photographer Rick Blacklaws. She's written another book privately and has had a hand in the creation of two books for the Museum of the Cariboo Chilcotin.

Diana's substantial history of community involvement, wherever she has lived in the Cariboo Chilcotin, is likely one of the reasons why she won one of the prestigious Queen's Fiftieth Anniversary Medals in 2002. "When you're my age you've had time to get involved in a lot of things," Diana says. "In the small communities everyone was active in everything. Bob helped build community skating rinks or whatever. I usually got involved because of family, or because I was mad about something and thought I could fix it. Occasionally I could."

For the last twenty years Diana and Bob have been active supporters of the Museum of the Cariboo Chilcotin. "I have been part, please note 'part,' of a small group of dedicated volunteers who started with practically no artifacts and less money and made the facility into what is considered to be one of the best 'small' museums in the province run by volunteers."

She says she got involved in the mid-1980s when it was a city museum, shared with the Tourist Info Centre. She was the first curator, volunteer of course, when it was taken over by the non-profit Williams Lake Museum and Historical Society and moved from Highway 97 to its present site on Fourth Avenue North, kitty-corner from the fire hall and city hall.

"I'm pretty well an artifact myself, as curator and a few years as society president."

When the museum was moved to its present location, she says there were few artifacts, so the board concentrated on developing a lot of written history displays.

"We have a lot of artifacts now thanks to community donations, but people like the written history so we still do it."

Teaching and parenting became a springboard for Diana into other educational and community activities. She was a founding member of the Columneetza Home School Committee which later became the PAC (Parents Advisory Committee). She served for four years on the School District 27 board, at different times chairing the finance, operating and education committees. While she was a trustee the board initiated the Indian Education and Rural Education programs which still exist today. During the 1970s Diana was a founding member of a Human Rights group that ran a street worker program and initiated the first Community Law Office in Williams Lake, which the province later took over.

In the 1990s Diana served six years on the board of the BC Open Learning Agency (now part of Thompson Rivers University), and on the Knowledge Network board. She has also served on many diverse boards and agencies at local, federal and provincial levels including the Salmonid Enhancement Committee, and the Spicer Commission. Diana had a hand in starting a women's shelter for the Cariboo Friendship Centre and youth groups. She also chaired the Association for Community Living board and the Cariboo Indian Training and Education Centre. She served on the city's centennial committee in 1971, and on the city's recreation commission, advisory planning committee, and museum committee.

While she is no longer involved, Diana served on the NDP provincial council both as a constituency and regional representative and on the Cariboo South Constituency executive.

"As far as I know, my husband and I are the only Williams Lake residents ever to have two sons on city council, and at the same time for fifteen years. Paul is a 'born' son, and Surinderpal Rathor, an informally adopted son.

Along with her volunteer work with the museum Diana currently chairs the Cariboo-Chilcotin Conservation Society, is a director on the Social Planning Council and a member of the city's Sustainability Committee. The current bee in her bonnet is concern over climate change and sustainability. With all that on her plate she plays duplicate bridge for fun.

Bob retired in 1988 after highway maintenance was privatized. The couple sold their larger family home in Williams Lake to one of their sons and moved into a trailer on the Stampede grounds to work as caretakers. After a couple of years at the Stampede grounds they bought a smaller, older home which keeps Bob busy with renovations. "There always seems to be something to do," says Bob, who celebrated his eightieth birthday in May 2008. "Especially in the garden."

Bob and Diana have enjoyed travelling and camping with their now large extended family, which includes eleven grandchildren ranging in age from two months to twenty-six years; plus three great-grandchildren. Son John and his family live in Fort St. John. Mike, Paul and Mark live in Williams Lake with their families. Bill and his family live in Port Coquitlam.

EDITOR'S NOTE:
This article appeared in *Casual Country*, 2008.

Jessie Frink

AUTOBIOGRAPHY

Life is a series of links in a chain of seemingly unrelated decisions and circumstances, which lead to one's current situation. Who would have ever dreamed that a daughter born to George and Olive Keeney on April 13, 1920, in the little town of Wren, Oregon, would be spending the last fifty-plus years of her life in the community of Big Lake, British Columbia?

This daughter, named Jessie Hazel after two maternal aunts, attended grade school in a little one-room school where there were never more than ten or twelve students. I started school at age four, a few weeks before my fifth birthday, along with my brother Ralph, who was a year and a half older. We and our classmates skipped the fifth grade. In the eighth grade there were four of us, and that comprised the entire school, which was closed after graduation.

With the teacher's blessing, Ralph and I skipped the last two or three months of school so we could herd cows along the gravelled country road. By this time our folks had separated and we lived with Mom, who was a farmer and kept a few Jersey cows as well as the usual chickens, turkeys and pigs. I learned to milk cows at age four, and had lots of practice while attending three different high schools, graduating at age sixteen. I was always thankful for this early start in the transition to adult life as I moved to Portland right after graduation where I lived with an older sister and attended business college. My career as a secretary and stenographer began in 1938 and led me to a number of different jobs—all interesting, varied and challenging to one who began as a little barefoot farm girl.

"It was all duck soup to me."

— JESSIE FRINK

The first solid link in the chain leading to Big Lake came with my decision to join the Women's Army Auxiliary Corps (WAAC) in early 1943. Basic training in Des Moines, Iowa, initiated me into snow and ice which was normal March weather there, but not common in western Oregon. We were invited to state a preference for the type of service that appealed to us the most, and I chose Motor Transport. Having grown up with a brother who began monkey-wrenching Model T Fords when he was twelve, it was all duck soup to me.

In August, 1943, the WAAC was taken into the regular army and became the Women's Army Corps (WAC). My first taste of minus twenty-five-degree Fahrenheit temperatures came in December before my request for a transfer to the Air Corps in Portland, Oregon, was approved. This proved to be another link in the chain leading to Big Lake. Mom was still farming at age sixty-six and I felt I should be closer since Ralph was also in the Army. Since there was no WAC Motor Corps in Portland, the next phase of my army career saw me back in the secretarial ranks. By the summer of 1945, the war was winding down and the WAC in Portland was shipped out. I spent my remaining Army time at an air base in Ephrata, Washington, where I spent V-E and V-J days.

After discharge in December, 1945, I could have had four years of college courtesy of the government, but I couldn't commit myself to that length of time pinching pennies to make ends meet, so I opted for a job in Salem as an insurance adjuster. Housing was short so I had room and board for $35 a month with a woman who wanted to rent her son's room while he was in the Navy.

The next step on my journey to Big Lake occurred when Carl Frink came home from the Navy to find his room occupied. His mom fixed a room in the basement for him. We soon began dating, and were married June 29, 1947.

Carl always wanted to go to Alaska, so we headed north on our honeymoon in a surplus Army Jeep and a sleeping trailer he had built. We had not reckoned with bumpy Canadian roads and after a few wrong turns and detours, we arrived in Calgary at Stampede time where the only accommodation was parking space in a farmer's field outside of town. By then the Jeep's front wheel had begun to wobble and we could see there was no way it could survive the distance to Alaska so the next day we headed south, without even taking in any Stampede events.

In May 1953, we decided to take a trip to Vancouver, BC. At that time, stores closed on various days and it was our luck to find upon arriving on a Tuesday evening that the main stores were closed on Wednesday. After breakfast that morning, we walked around the block and in the window of a little real estate office, Carl noticed a picture of a man on horseback in the middle of a meadow with the grass reaching up to his stirrups. As it happened, the real estate dealer was in his office and directed us to the couple in Abbotsford who owned the property. Their description of the area plus more pictures convinced Carl it was utopia.

Five months later we set out for Big Lake. We found it a bit daunting when we ran out of pavement north of Hope, but we kept on and made it to Lac la Hache where we rented a cabin. Being October, the nights were frosty and we had never heard of antifreeze, but luckily the car wasn't badly frozen and no harm done. We went into Williams Lake and had breakfast at the old Ranch Café. I told Carl we'd better have them put up a lunch for us, but he said, "Oh, no—there'll be some place to eat out there."

We were to contact Gus Adams, who owned a place at Big Lake, who would take us to see the section of property we were interested in, three miles off the main road. It was a gorgeous fall day, the 22nd of October, and we walked down this wagon trail through the woods carpeted with golden aspen leaves. It was bewitching and Carl was more and more interested. Much of the place was timbered, some fir but mostly spruce and aspen, with quite a large area of native hay meadow and about twenty acres of cleared land. It turned out that Gus Adams wanted to sell his place, which had frontage on Big Lake so we decided to think about all the possibilities over the winter and come back in the spring to see it in another season.

Of course we soon discovered there was not a café around the bend, but Mrs. Adams came to our rescue with some cold pancakes, explaining that her arthritis was so bad she could no longer knead bread, so they made enough pancakes in the morning to last through the day. She was a lovely and gracious woman.

We made our second trip to the Cariboo in April 1954 and probably saw it at its worst with snow on the ground and freezing nights. On this trip we were accompanied by Bert Anderson, owner of the section we were interested in. He had helped build the Silverhorn Lodge, which had been operated as a dude ranch, and was familiar with their string of horses so was able to catch and saddle three and we had a mounted tour of the land.

In his mind, Carl saw the fields he would clear all covered with a bountiful hay crop. I was less enthusiastic, but told him if that was the way he wanted to make a living, it was okay with me but not to expect me to be a farm hand. Talk about famous last words!

We signed agreements to purchase the Anderson section and the Adams place. We hoped to adopt children and I knew there was no way I wanted to live three miles from the main road with no power or phone. The only building on the section was a one-room log cabin, which Anderson had built while proving up on his land claim. The Adams house, while not finished inside, had three rooms and would be liveable.

Our purchase of the two properties was concluded in the fall of 1954, and Carl brought the first load of machinery up in March of 1955. He worked on finishing the inside of the house with Gyproc and building kitchen cupboards. Mrs. Adams had dealt with orange crates stacked for shelves, with a curtain in front. They had moved to the place in 1920, living in a tent through two winters before moving into a house. Talk about pioneers—the winters were much colder back then also. They told us January was the coldest month but it usually warmed up to zero degrees Fahrenheit every day.

Carl returned to Salem in July and we loaded up our household goods, including an Ashley thermostatically controlled wood heater, a wood cookstove, and a propane refrigerator. That truck was so fully loaded, it would not have held one additional item. The Plymouth sedan was packed as well, but there was room for my pet cat, Ichabod, and my older sister Molly, who wanted to see where the two adventurers were headed.

We reached the border at Sumas in the late afternoon and were very fortunate we didn't have to unload anything. We actually were perfectly legal except for a box of my favourite houseplants that were concealed in the middle of the load. The road through the Fraser Canyon had not yet been improved so it was a slow grind up all the hills. Carl was ahead, but after we were through the canyon he told me to go on ahead, then later laughed at how fast I had sped up and left him in the dust.

Highway 97 was in the process of being straightened and paved, with various seven-mile stretches in the different stages of development. Some sections were the original gravel road, some sections were built up with a rock base on top, and some were levelled off ready for paving. We did make it to Big Lake that day, after staying in Abbotsford the night before—our first as landed immigrants to Canada.

In addition to his carpentry work, Carl made time to work up the cleared land and plant oats, which made good winter feed for the twenty heifer calves we bought at a sale in November. There was eight inches of snow; the gravel road hadn't been graded, and we almost didn't make it up some of the steep hills hauling our girls home. We kept them in the yard around the house the first winter, as it was the only fenced area. For a few days, we had to drive them down to Big Lake Creek for water, and chasing them around in the snow wearing summer boots at minus twenty degrees Fahrenheit. I wondered why anyone would want to live in such a place. It seemed much better after I purchased winter boots.

As I had grown up with wood stoves for heat and cooking, it didn't take too long to get back into the routine of knowing how to keep the oven at the right temperature for baking. That first fall while Carl was busy farming, I would spend a couple hours every day picking blueberries and canned over thirty quarts plus made jam and pies. They are

Reflections: Then and Now

An old man sat on his cabin porch
Rocking to and fro
His mind turned back on a winding track
To the days of long ago,
While the waters of Big Lake lapped the shore
As they had for untold years
And the lonesome call of a loon rang out –
It was music to his ears.
When lights around the lake came on
In the dusk of the setting sun
He remembered the hiss of the old gas lamp
And the chug of light plants starting one by one.
The telephone rang and he knew it was his
No more a muffled "two shorts and a long"
That everyone answered with honest concern
To see "Is anything wrong?"
A car sped by on the smooth paved road
But it was not always so –
There were years of gravel and dust and mud
He was happy to see them go.
In the early days he knew each car
And the friend behind the wheel;
They'd often stop for a coffee break
Or maybe a hurried meal.
But times had changed and people too
Not always, he thought, for the best
There was little time for visiting now
And he was just like the rest.
Those calls that brightened the days gone by
Were gone like the leaves in fall
And now the folks who lived next door
You hardly knew at all.
He thought of the price of his supper steak
And whistled under his breath
Were it not for game in those "good old days"
A guy coulda' starved to death
For the steers he'd sold at two bits a pound
Had barely paid off the bank.
In his mind he pictured the crops he'd raised
And the long hard years of toil
He'd spent to clear the willows and spruce
From the fertile virgin soil.
The days of old were memories now
Some were bad and some good
There was no way he could bring them back
And he wouldn't if he could.
Yes, the good old days were memories now
And 'twas best to leave them so
For whether the times were good or bad
The years would still come and go.

—J. Frink

From Top: Jessie Keeney (Frink) stands by her jeep while serving in the Women's Army Auxiliary Corps during World War II in Des Moines, Iowa.

Jessie and Carl Frink leaving Oregon with their truck loaded to the brim bound for British Columbia and their new home at Big Lake.

Jessie Frink at home with her cat, Buffy, in Big Lake.

not that easy to find anymore; in fact, I haven't picked any for many years.

The old Big Lake Ranch across the creek from our place had been an overnight stopping place for men hauling freight to the goldfields around Likely and Quesnel Forks. The barn was built to house fifty horses, and the house had ten bedrooms. Jim and Ruth Wannop purchased the place and moved there in 1955, the same year we arrived.

There were several small portable mills operating in the area, so they started a grocery store to supply the mill workers. Pat Harmon, a school teacher, and her husband Ken lived in a cabin on the Wannop place at the time, and I suggested to Pat and Ruth, who also had experience teaching, that if they wanted to teach Sunday School we could have it at our place. The idea met with approval and was well attended for several years. Those were the days before anyone had electricity, and there wasn't as much for kids to do as there is now. We had wiener roasts every month in the summer. After I began working in town in 1965, Pat Harmon taught a Bible lesson during lunch hour at school for a number of years. The Wannops had moved away by this time.

We found all the neighbours very friendly and accepting of us from the beginning. When we were given a hind quarter of venison a little before the season opened, we knew we were "in." That first fall, Carl went moose hunting and thought he was lucky to find a large bull in target range until he had it dressed out and found it was so tough it wasn't good for anything but hamburger. It was even difficult to put it through the hand grinder. We ate a lot of meatloaf that winter.

We only had the truck for transportation. Its heater didn't work and a little catalytic heater did well to keep a spot open in front of the driver so he could see out the windshield, so a trip to town was an adventure. We only made a trip once a month, so if you forgot something it was a long wait.

For the first few years our mail was delivered in a bag hung on the gatepost. On the return trip the next day they would pick up the bag with outgoing mail. Delivery was once a week in winter and twice a week in summer.

Many stories have been written about ranch life in the Cariboo and the challenges people faced. I'm sure ours was not much different. I was more fortunate than some women in that we had a generator that would operate my Easy spin-dry washer. Carl had installed a sink with a drain into a rock pit so I only had to carry the water in from a pump on the porch—except when the pump froze at minus fifty degrees Fahrenheit and it was necessary to chop a hole in the ice and pack forty buckets a couple hundred feet uphill to the house.

We were approved to adopt children and prepared for the first one offered to us—an adorable three-month-old boy—even to borrowing a crib and buying clothing. But after some delay the mother decided to keep him. The next time they had a baby for us I was in Oregon following a death in the family. In this particular case they couldn't wait as the baby had to be taken right from the hospital. I've always felt the Lord knows best, and consoled myself with the thought that while we missed the joys of raising children, we also missed the heartaches some parents encounter.

Life became a lot easier when hydro power came to Big Lake in 1966. One of the biggest advantages was being able to plug in block heaters in the winter.

The summer of 1964 changed our methods of putting up food for the stock. It rained nearly every day, making it impossible to put up hay, so we bought a chopper and Carl dug a silage pit. It was while driving truck alongside the chopper that I decided that was not the way I wanted to spend the rest of my life. So the next spring I returned to office life. Two years working at the *Tribune* in the old building on Oliver Street and thirteen for the Carlsons at Williams Lake Building Supply. I stayed in town during the week, returning home Friday nights with a load of kids from the Dorm.

Weekends were busy as Carl had been thrown from his horse and almost broke his neck. It healed somewhat but he couldn't stand the jar of riding, so I did the range riding during the summers as long as we had the ranch. I also tried to prepare some food ahead so he didn't have to depend on batching. It was difficult for both of us but the extra income helped.

Carl's family had a history of diabetes and when he began losing weight and displaying some of the other classic symptoms in the late 1960s, it didn't take long to discover the cause. Local doctors tried to treat him with medication but it was not until he saw a specialist in Vancouver and began taking insulin that he was able to control it. We put the ranch on the market and sold the farmland in March 1973. Carl had begun building a new house on the Big Lake property in 1971, which by that time really felt like home, so we kept it.

Carl began experiencing leg pains, and was finally diagnosed with myeloma (bone cancer). His life was downhill from then on, with periods of feeling better when the chemo took effect, but there was no cure and he came to the end of the line in February 1988, two weeks after his seventy-first birthday. He never lost his love for the land and the work he put into it. He remarked one time, "All I ever got out of that place was hard work, but I loved every minute of it."

A lifelong faith in God saw me through some difficult times along the way. All the decisions I've made have not been the best, and not necessarily what I would do if I could turn back the pages of time, but I can truthfully say that the road I have travelled has been worth it for the friends I've known. This is a community of wonderful, supportive people and I can't imagine wanting to be anywhere else the rest of my life.

Hazel Huckvale

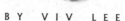

BY VIV LEE

Mother: a person who sees that there are only four pieces of pie to share among five persons and promptly remarks that she never cared for pie. If she says so, don't tell her she's wrong although she often, very often, enjoys a lively argument. In this case, she'll make you understand that she has a right to relish her self-denial of the pie or whatever else she wants to share. "That's my nature," she admits.

The word mother, whose true definition encompasses the virtues of love and unselfish sharing, has been deservedly bestowed on Hazel Huckvale. In over fifty years of service as a teacher, friend, advisor, and community builder, Hazel was recognized as the caring mother of Williams Lake. It was Maureen Tickner, president of the Seniors Housing Society, who proposed this fitting description at Hazel's civic eightieth birthday party.

Born on July 24, 1913, of Scottish parents in Alexandria, Ontario, Hazel was raised on her father's dairy farm. Her mother was a teacher. Although Hazel enjoyed the outdoor life, she looked forward to her move to Williams Lake in 1953. She said she loved it from day one.

The people of Williams Lake, a closely knit community, may disagree on many things, but they all seem to agree on the goodness of Hazel Huckvale and her untiring work for their community. In Hazel's declining years, her good friend Maureen said:

"She is one frail-looking woman with fearless willpower and determination to get things done for this little place she calls home."

Hazel's granddaughter, Tara, must have inherited her fearlessness in speaking her mind. About Hazel she says: "Oh boy, was she stubborn. Opinionated and welcomed an argument, but I loved her. She taught me to stand up for what I think is right in spite of tough opposition."

Hazel's civic contributions began when she ran for city council and won at age sixty-seven. She served with passionate zeal for nine years. She was involved in building three seniors housing complexes and was admired for her active leadership in their organization from planning to completion. That was Hazel's way of doing things: "You start a job, you finish it." From experience, her colleagues and the general public discovered that she was obstacle-proof when it came to getting things done against great odds.

Hazel Huckvale attends a potluck dinner. Hazel went to many social functions and fundraisers during her more than half century of life in Williams Lake.

Left: Portrait of Hazel Huckvale by painter Mildred Jane Baines.

Since she was eighteen years old, Hazel wanted to utilize her innate ability to organize and so she joined the Liberal Party. At ninety-one she was still an active party member. So highly did Prime Minister Pierre Trudeau value her civic consciousness, he invited her to become a senator in his government, but Hazel declined. She preferred to stay close to the people she loved.

Today Williams Lake enjoys an inner city bus system as well as a Go Pass for seniors thanks to the hard work of Hazel. Being a senior herself, she said she could closely relate to the needs of the older generation. Her Christian goodness continued with her inspiring activity with St. Andrew's United Church.

People say she was born to be of service to others. "I just feel happy to be with people, especially those I can help," Hazel would say. As the elder counsellor at the Seniors Centre for over sixteen years, Hazel advised seniors about getting their legal benefits; she helped them with tax returns, comforted them in their sorrow and sickness, and played the role of mother to those in need of a kind word, an embrace, and most of all a helping hand.

Her detractors, and they were few, didn't always agree with her aggressive and sometimes unconventional style, but Hazel would dismiss it as water off a duck's back. "I enjoy criticism, especially when we can argue sensibly about it," she liked to say. "Don't give me my own way or agree with me because you think I am old. Just admit I am right."

Those who knew her well would take this bit of arrogance as a small part of an enigmatic character. Her natural ability to confront opposition with logic and reason could be unnerving to those who couldn't see the soundness of her argument. They claim that for Hazel Huckvale there were only two sides of a story: "Her side, and the wrong side." She would disagree, of course.

Her background gave Hazel a head start against those who could not lay claim, like she could, to holding a Bachelor of Arts degree from Ottawa University and both a BA and master's in Education from the University of British Columbia. Furthermore, her experience as a teacher from the youthful age of seventeen in Ontario, followed by a period of twenty-five years as principal of Glendale Elementary School in Williams Lake surely gave her an advantage in fashioning her "Hazel-perfect" premise.

According to her granddaughter, Tara, Hazel was a stickler for proper use of the English language. "She was very picky about grammar and could drive a person crazy with her corrections. She thought she was still a school principal." She might have been guilty of scaring some of her students, as well as most of her teachers, but the unanimous verdict is that she was an inspiring principal.

When psychologists say that out of sorrow, greater strength can evolve, we think of Hazel Huckvale's natural, caring spirit being further empowered with the tragedy of losing the two men she loved most. First her husband Jim, then later her son, Neil, in a plane crash. Her readiness to volunteer for service seemed to increase after her tragic losses.

Age was no handicap. At least Hazel didn't let it bother her. "I take one day at a time and do my best," she would say. Public opinion is that Hazel always liked to have her fingers in every pie. She detested being late or "out of the loop," as she called it. She also disliked cooking and housekeeping. Simply put, these mundane duties got in her way of being able to serve the community. She was happiest when people, especially seniors, sought her help and advice.

Her popularity was sometimes a humbug for those going on a shopping trip with her. Tara remembers ruefully, "She stopped to speak to everybody. As a child, this was a dreaded experience for me. It was the same reaction from Grandpa Jim. He would complain but in vain. She had to listen to everybody's problems, offer solutions, and sometimes even get into full-blown arguments. Especially in a party of close friends, Hazel never missed an opportunity to banter words. Sometimes, mischievously, she would make a statement with a deliberate error and argue strongly in its favour. When the others became frustrated, she playfully confessed that it was her practical joke and the party would erupt in laughter."

Hazel Huckvale and her husband Jim were still sweethearts in their old age.

Her penchant for shocking behaviour "not befitting an old lady according to the rules of convention," used to upset her granddaughter as a child. Even at the end Tara enjoyed crossing swords with Hazel, even in public. It was all good-natured, although the public sometimes looked askance at them in disapproval. They couldn't understand a young person being so argumentative with an old lady, but Hazel enjoyed their discomfort. "I guess I still like being a little imp," Tara says.

Over the years Hazel bonded with thousands of school children and seniors into a non-racial surrogate family, which included the Sikh community who made her a Charter Member of their temple for teaching their members how to raise funds in Canada. Six years after arriving in Williams Lake, Hazel saw the need and organized English as a Second Language for immigrants from India, teaching the men during their lunch breaks at the mills and the women in the mornings. She obviously meant it when she said, "I love all people and nature."

Hazel's story would be incomplete without input from her friend of thirty years, Maureen Tickner. They first met at a sing-along for seniors at which the talented Hazel played the piano and led the singing. Every Wednesday afternoon she entertained at Cariboo Lodge. For over eighteen years, through snowy winters and into springtime, she lifted the spirits of seniors with her renditions of their favourite songs, reviving memories of wartime and romance.

With her infectious smile and colourful hats, gaudily decorated with ribbons, jewellery and flowers, and matching dress and shoes, Hazel was a picture of genuine happiness.

Adding a touch of blush to her cheeks, she would say, "When you dress up, it shows the world that you also care about them."

After twenty-five years of memorable service as a principal of Glendale Elementary School, Hazel was appointed seniors counsellor by the Ministry Responsible for Seniors. She considered it a great honour that gave her the opportunity to help thousands of seniors for over seventeen years without an official office. "Any quiet spot was good enough to do a good deed."

> *"When you dress up it shows the world you care."*
>
> — HAZEL HUCKVALE

Maureen Tickner speaks of enjoying Hazel's story of Bill, a resident of the Lodge, throwing his whiskey bottle out the second-floor window and hiding his six packs of beer in the toilet tank; a Cariboo cowboy trick. She loved to share a funny story so much that a stranger wouldn't believe she was a stern teacher and a serious city counsellor.

Laughing at herself was nothing new to Hazel. At a serious finance meeting, she once turned up impeccably dressed except for wearing conspicuously mismatched knee-high stockings. She willingly exposed the spectacle to the hilarious reaction of the other members, made even more enjoyable by her assumed sangfroid.

"Hazel had a big heart. She taught me that the greatest thing in life is to help others," Maureen says, noting that Hazel declared that her volunteer work had given her the best years of her life. "If we all followed Hazel's shining example, what a wonderful world it would be. No wonder I considered her as the ever-loving Mother of Williams Lake."

In 2001, Mayor Ivan Bonnell presented Hazel with the first gold key to the City of Williams Lake. At every level—federal, provincial, and municipal—Hazel has been honoured. Prime Minister Paul Martin, then finance minister, paid tribute to her indomitable courage in getting things done against all odds when he told her, "You've never walked away from a challenge." Her records prove it.

Perhaps her most cherished recognition was the naming of the Glendale gymnasium, the Hazel Huckvale Auditorium. In it, there will be lots of fun, action and noise, characteristics of Hazel who had to fight (verbally) with lots of noise and action to get things done. "I loved every minute of it," she would say.

Hazel must surely have drunk from the fountain of youth and at that special faucet which is the source of her love and compassion. She admitted, however, that she was just one person. "There are many more like me who have done as much as I have but maybe not as noisily." In dealing with officials, Hazel knew the ropes. Her advice was: go to the top. "It doesn't matter which party is in power," she would say.

Contacting civic leaders, premiers, and the prime minister came naturally to Hazel, who amazed others with her audacity. Ottawa knew her persistence. "It's no wonder that she loved to discuss politics in all shapes and forms; she was especially knowledgeable in Aboriginal affairs, notably about the Shuswap, Tsilhqot'in, and Carrier Bands," says Maureen Tickner, who loved Hazel as a mentor. "I attribute most of my success to Hazel's advice and example," Maureen continues. "I looked forward to our regular debates about our mutual interest in God and His goodness. Even on such a serious subject as spirituality she couldn't help being light-hearted. She would say she wasn't afraid of dying, but was afraid that heaven may be too quiet for her."

Maureen says she assured Hazel that God and the angels would keep her busy bringing friends and families together and teaching the little angels the Queen's English. "I told her that heaven would indeed be busy with her around, but her friends on earth would miss her."

When Hazel Huckvale came to Williams Lake in 1955, it was mainly a backward, dirt-road village with many households without power and hardly any amenities. Today the city is a thriving community with a positive outlook and services for its citizens, especially its seniors. Much of this progress can be attributed to Hazel, super senior, whom everyone called the Mother of Williams Lake.

Hazel passed away in August 2006, at the age of ninety-three.

Biddy Jones

BY GAEIL FARRAR

Biddy Jones is petrified to get up on stage and act, but behind the scenes she's a real tiger. She has been honing her theatre craft for thirty some years and in 2004 won the prestigious Hamber Award from Theatre BC for her efforts.

She is also a very proud mother and grandmother and long-time advocate for the poor and underprivileged in society. She vents this side of her outspoken personality through her work for the New Democratic Party, and credits her eclectic lifestyle to a very forward-thinking mother. "My mother was the biggest influence in my life although I didn't know it at the time. As kids we had a lot of freedom. She was not the average parson's wife, I'll tell you that."

Biddy was born in Kelowna on April 15, 1929, to Charles and Eve Davis. Her father was Rector of St. Michael's and All Angel's Anglican Church in Kelowna. He was very musical, played the organ and conducted the choir. Growing up during the depression Biddy says her mother supplemented her father's income by renting rooms. "Once we had two prostitutes staying in the back bedroom while the Bishop stayed in the front bedroom. There were goats and horses in our back yard."

Still she says life was pretty normal. "I just lived such an ordinary life. In those days we all did. I didn't have a job. I didn't want one. In the 1950s you had to get married by twenty-three or you were considered an old maid."

So typical of many women at that time, Biddy married her high school sweetheart, John (Joto), who coincidentally had the same last name of Davis, but was no relation. "We told Joto's mother we were going to be married and she said 'that's ridiculous' so we eloped," says Biddy, who was only eighteen years old when they skipped across the border and got married on New Year's Eve in 1948 at the famous Hitching Post in Coeur d'Alene, Idaho. "The only thing I wanted out of life was to be married and to have a family."

They settled in Kimberley where Joto got a good-paying job working at the Sullivan Mine. Jan, the first of their four children, was born there in 1950. Then the family moved to Nelson where Joto became a travelling salesman, selling waterless cookers. "Meanwhile we

Biddy Jones and her oldest daughter, Jan, on horseback in the early 1950s.

lived on homemade soup and homemade bread," Biddy says.

Cooking from scratch wasn't much of a hardship because Biddy loved to cook and still regularly makes homemade soup and bread, albeit these days with the help of a bread-maker. Son Ian was born in Nelson in 1953, and a year or so later they moved to Deep Cove where their daughter Kim was born in 1955 in North Vancouver.

Biddy says it was a wretched time because they had little money and lived in a house with a stream running under the foundation and mould growing in the cupboards. "I went skiing a few times in North Vancouver. You just did it because it was sort of fun to do, but I never got good at it."

Youngest daughter, Nicola, was born in 1960 after the family had moved back to Kelowna. Having a travelling salesman for a husband meant Biddy spent a lot of time on her own with the children, some of it quite frightening in those early post-war years. "In those days we were so scared. Kids were being trained to go under their desks when air raid sirens went off. I remember being terrified that a plane flying overhead in the middle of the night was an enemy bomber."

And there were other consequences. In 1964, after sixteen years of marriage and four children, Biddy discovered that her husband was living a separate and very romantic life of his own on the road. "It was so typical, a note in the pocket of a jacket going to the

An artist on many fronts Biddy Jones takes some time to do some painting in an outdoor setting.

cleaners," Biddy says. "I believe he had been getting away with it for years. He told one woman I was a show girl from Las Vegas and didn't know how to look after the kids properly. I tried to convince him to become a real estate agent but he didn't pass the exam. Now I see that he may very well have failed the exam because he didn't want to get off the road and settle down."

She can joke about it now but at the time, the break-up was devastating. Biddy gave Joto the option of changing his ways or leaving. He left. She says he wasn't a complete cad. "He sent one paycheque home a month, and I got the house and the mortgage."

A year later, Biddy sold the house she and Joto had built together and she and the kids moved in with her mother. Biddy's father had died when she was fifteen, so her mother was on her own running a riding stable on the outskirts of Kelowna that was known as Mrs. D's. Her attic became a haven for the kids. Biddy got a job at the Kelowna library and set about the task of building a home for her family on her mother's property. "I always enjoyed people who build things," says Biddy.

"You make a conscious decision. I had one life to live and I was going to be as happy as I could," says Biddy. "I looked after the kids, worked at the library and thinned the apples in the orchard." But in the back of her mind she knew she wanted to remarry again someday.

Biddy met her second husband, Dave Jones, through one of her best friends from high school who thought they might be well suited for each other. Betty Carlson lived in Williams Lake and worked for Canada Manpower, where Dave also worked as a job planner and counsellor. One day Biddy loaded three of her children into the car and headed north to Williams Lake to meet him. Unfortunately the fates had other plans when her car broke down at Cache Creek.

"I was sitting by the side of the road crying. My son Ian said 'everything will be alright' and that kind of cheered me up. The road wasn't paved. It was dusty and dirty. Finally an American came along and rescued us, and we returned home to Kelowna."

Undaunted, Biddy's friend made a second attempt to put Dave and Biddy together about a year later. By then, Dave was working for Manpower in Revelstoke. "Betty kept bugging him until he called me. He came down to Kelowna and picked me up at the library and we hit it off really well."

A few months later they went to Mexico together in a camper for a few weeks. They had a good time, but by the time Biddy got back home she wasn't really sure if she wanted to get married again. But Dave continued to pursue her.

"He wrote me love letters that would just scorch the paper they were written on. They were so hot I burned them all. I was so embarrassed to keep them."

They dated for a year when they had time to get together, then decided to tie the knot. "In a second marriage you are a little more tolerant about what you will accept and a little more leery too. Dave was known as the old guy with the grey beard. He was forty-eight and I was forty. He said he would never marry anyone with kids and he ended up with me and my brood. I was quite sexy in those days," Biddy jokes.

Dave was also divorced with three boys, Ted, Paul, and Peter, who were living with their mother in Vancouver. Over the years Dave and Biddy managed to share time with all seven of their children and eventually their grandchildren, as their blended family grew and branched out with children of their own.

Dave and Biddy shared one great passion—a love for politics and in particular the NDP. "We were both considered a bit nuts because we both supported the NDP," says Biddy. "Most people in those days were Socreds or Liberal or Conservative. In the 1960s, during the cold war I belonged to the Voice of Women started by Dr. Helen Caldicott. Many prominent women were members and we would write letters, and hold meetings in effort to end the cold war and the war in Vietnam. The thing I remember is that we would get letters back on the new and official line from government contradicting what we were finding. We were told we were radicals who were just being sucked into this, but sure enough, years later, we were proved right."

Biddy says her own parents were very apolitical, so when she first became politically involved she scrutineered for the Liberals and voted Social Credit. "I didn't realize this wasn't done."

Then in her thirties she met a friend who was a strong socialist. "We would argue for hours. Everything I said, he would try to convince me I was on the wrong track completely. I suddenly realized that what he was saying was my philosophy in life. It was what I believed."

She says getting involved with the NDP was a thankless task of telephoning people, organizing potluck dinners and endlessly trying to raise money. "You have an election and spend the next four years trying to pay off the debt."

The hard work finally paid off on August 30, 1972, shortly after Dave and Biddy moved to Williams Lake, when the NDP was elected to govern British Columbia for the first time. "I remember that night. I was scrutineering at Kwaleen Elementary and we were losing dismally as usual. I got home and opened the door and the news was on television and Dave said we were winning. It was a real high point in my life."

Biddy first developed an interest in theatre while she and Dave were still living in Revelstoke and she joined a little theatre group there. Her interest continued to blossom when they moved to Williams Lake in the early 1970s. At first she tried acting, but soon discovered she suffered from horrendous stage fright. Undaunted she started working behind the scenes and found that she had a talent for directing.

Biddy considers her biggest achievement the production of Canadian plays and introducing new talent to the theatre. She particularly enjoys working with children and has introduced many children to the theatre over the years through her plays and workshops. "Although a lot of my plays have pushed the envelope and had serious themes, the icing on the cake for me was the children's plays and working with young people."

She directed plays for Kids Stuff theatre in Boitanio Park, and for several summers she headed out to Wineglass Ranch near Riske Creek in the Chilcotin, to put on workshops for children. There the sets were built with hay bales, the curtains were the sweeping branches of a huge willow tree, and the backdrop was the sight of bighorn sheep on the cliff-tops. One of her favourite kids' productions was an abbreviated version of Shakespeare's *A Midsummer Night's Dream*, which they began creating at Wineglass Ranch and ended up performing at Williams Lake Secondary School. "I often wonder what the Bard would have thought of this raggle-taggle band of young thespians doing one of his most popular plays. I think he would have said: 'Right on!'"

During the past thirty years, Biddy has produced and directed more than thirty plays for the Studio Theatre Society in Williams Lake, usually about one a year. Whenever she could she would direct plays by Canadian playwrights. "Done well they are 'us' and people love them," she says.

Jen King

BY GLORIA ATAMANENKO

Jen Pawlyshyn King was born in Edmonton of Ukrainian immigrant parents who came to Canada in 1910. During the 1920s her father was always away from home working as a coal miner in the Alberta foothills. A man well ahead of his times in his interest in nature and nutrition, he picked boxes of blueberries in his after-work hours to bring home to his family. Jen's mother preserved them for winter.

Raising six children on a coal miner's salary was difficult during the depression years of the 1930s, but Jen's parents met the challenge with determination, ingenuity and hard work. Her mother grew vegetables on their well-cultivated city lot and stored them for winter use, and grew flowers to brighten the family's spirits and their home. She taught her children a love of beauty and ways of bringing it to various facets of everyday life. "Does it take much more time to make things look neat and pretty?" she asked her children, and showed by example that it does not. Now, when Jen serves a plate of cookies with her delicate, aromatic cups of tea, it holds lovely surprises—flowers, sprigs of fresh berries, or herbs—a delight for the eyes as well as for the palate.

The family struggled to learn English; there was no special help like English as a Second Language (ESL) for immigrants in those days. They also treasured their own language and rich cultural heritage of song and dance. Jen and her sisters and brother

Jen King and her son, Mike, sharing a laugh.

walked at least three miles to a Ukrainian cultural centre to learn to read, write, and sing in Ukrainian, and to dance Ukrainian folk dances. Jen loved music, and learned to play the mandolin so well that she was invited to join a Ukrainian string orchestra that toured Alberta. She was deeply moved when performing for rural audiences when she saw the tears of joy in the eyes of many people. Jen dearly loved ballet, and during World War II she was a member of a dance company that entertained the troops.

Always an avid reader and learner, Jen graduated from high school with honours in history and English. "The principal called me into his office," she recalls, "and advised me to change my surname if I wanted to get anywhere in life." Such an attitude to non-Anglo-Saxons was not unusual in those days. Throughout their years at school, she and her siblings felt they were considered "Bohunks." In the seventy years since that time, Jen has seen many positive changes including the growth of respect and appreciation for the multicultural composition of Canadian society. She has travelled widely in Canada, as well as in other parts of the world, and is delighted by the variety and quality of creative talent she has seen. An enthusiastic member of the Council of Canadians, she reads widely and intensively about Canada's national affairs and its place and role in a complex and changing world.

After high school, Jen studied accounting and worked for a chartered accountant and in various other business settings. Later, in married life, she helped her husband Harry in their business with her accounting experience. After his untimely death in 1978, Jen became president of their company, White Saddle Air Services, and managed the business for many years, even working sixteen- to eighteen-hour days sometimes. Dealing with banks and aviation officials was not easy for a woman in those days, but she won confidence, admiration, and respect.

As an eight-year-old during the Depression in Edmonton, Jen accompanied her father when he attended a peaceful workers' demonstration protesting against unfair labour practices. She witnessed a policeman's baton descending upon a worker's head. The memory of that incident raised lifelong questions and challenges for her; she became concerned about how to balance the demands of running a business with principles of social justice and community needs.

Jen met Harry King in Shaughnessy Hospital in Vancouver, where she volunteered, and where he was an out-patient war veteran. They shared many experiences and values: growing up as children of immigrant parents; appreciation of close, supportive family relationships; self-reliance and hard work; and an entrepreneurial spirit. They also enjoyed travel and felt a deep commitment to Canada. They married, and as part of their work and also for pleasure, they travelled Canada "from coast, to coast, to coast," with a fly-in up the Mackenzie River to Tuktoyaktuk. They made sure that all of their three sons, Dave, Mike and Brian, had a chance to travel across Canada, from Victoria to Newfoundland.

In 1968 on a holiday trip from Victoria to Bella Coola, Jen, Harry, and their three children visited the West Branch (of the Homathko River) Valley, south of Tatla Lake. They fell in love with the beautiful mountain valley, which slopes down from 3,000 feet to sea level at Bute Inlet, and is flanked by towering Mount Waddington on its western side. The Kings acquired land on Bluff Lake, visited and worked on it every year, and when the children became youths, the family decided to move there.

By 1977, they obtained a licence to operate an aviation service on the basis of providing for "public convenience and necessity." The transportation provided by White Saddle Air Services has facilitated work in many areas: forestry, fire fighting, mining exploration, drill moves, aerial surveys, timber cruising, water surveys, medical services, cattle spotting, filming, and recreational activities such as mountain climbing, wilderness hiking, and alpine photography. For over a quarter of a century the company has been a valuable resource for the local community, the region, and for scientists and mountaineers visiting from different parts of the world.

> *"When I walk in the woods, even the trees nod a hello."*
>
> — JEN KING

Building an aviation base in the wilderness without electricity or water and "using minimal equipment like wheelbarrows and muscle" required family dedication and

Jen King stands in front of the White Saddle Bell Jet Ranger helicopter with her grandchildren.

commitment to hard, hard work. It started with Harry and Jen and continues with their sons, daughters-in-law, and grandchildren to the present.

For Jen, the beauty of the mountain valley and the opportunity to observe wild creatures who live there has always been revitalizing and precious. She wrote to a business colleague; "From my windows, I can watch the magnificent trumpeter swans perform their ballet on the lake, see the eagles soar and dive for dinner, or watch the deer grazing on the runway, and in winter I can watch the coyotes or wolves skate across the lake."

But nature is not always benign. One morning Jen was charged by a deer who resented the interruption of its feast in Jen's garden. Jen sprinted to the safety of her home. The wolves and coyotes lured son Brian's beautiful dog, Kolo, onto the ice and killed him. The narrow road along Bluff Lake gets treacherously icy in winter. Most sinister of all, a heavy fog bank at sea level led to Harry's fatal helicopter accident.

On August 1, 1978, Harry headed off from Bluff Lake in his Bell-47 helicopter for a routine maintenance on Vancouver Island, a distance of less than one hundred nautical miles. The weather was calm on that summer day and when Harry encountered a thick fog bank at the mouth of Knight Inlet and after setting down on a sand bar for an hour or two, he decided to push through it. He was never heard from again though the tail fin was recovered in the water near Port Hardy by searchers as they combed the waters looking for the missing pilot. Son David also found two White Saddle gas cans that Harry carried on the rack of the helicopter for spare gas. Both sons, David and Mike, borrowed airplanes to carry on looking for their father after the official search ended.

The loss of a loving husband, business partner, and closest friend was a devastating blow to Jen. The simplest, easiest course of action could have been for her to return to the urban conveniences and cultural riches of Victoria, but Jen was never attracted to the easiest courses of action.

Comforted by the knowledge that Harry would have been proud of her and placing the needs of her family foremost, she managed the aviation business they had built up with their three sons. White Saddle Air Services developed a reputation for excellent performance. One pleased customer described it as excelling "beyond the norms expected even by the international mountaineering society." Another client wrote, "Many thanks to the King family for Jen's world-famous hospitality, the bonus flights with Dave, and the dependable, smooth chopper rides with Mike." Jen herself comments, "I give credit to my sons David, Michael, Brian, and their wonderful wives Lori, Audrey, and Chris."

Sons Michael and David and their families work in the aviation business and live in the West Branch Valley. Son Brian and his family now farm and work in southern Alberta. Jen is a passionate advocate for farmers. "Food doesn't come from plastic cartons," she once wrote, "Many folks are not aware of that. Producers rarely hit the headlines, and manipulators of funds, etc. have become the so-called backbone of our society. Agriculture Canada is becoming a micro-chip producer...try eating them!"

Jen's own garden is beautifully laid out and brimming with healthy veggies. Her greenhouse was the first of its kind in the West Chilcotin. Its produce nourishes family, visitors, and friends. Her flowers brighten tired days, and her berries, hardy apples, and plums provide feasts not only for humans but for birds and much larger wildlife!

Over the years Jen has delighted in watching and encouraging the development of her eight grandchildren from babyhood to young adulthood. In spring of 2009 she was blessed by the birth of her first great-granddaughter. "What could be more nourishing," she asks, "than listening to a sweet, innocent, unbiased child? If you want to learn something, ask a child, but listen to what he or she says."

Jen's approach towards her sons and their wives and children suggests a valuable model for harmonious family relationships. "I have a wonderful family," she says, "and I love them all, but I will not trespass on their territory unless I am invited." In deeply caring and sharing her ways she has encouraged and helped Michael and David and their wives in the aviation business. She has been equally supportive of Brian and Chris in their farming and business ventures in Alberta.

Jen's caring and nurturing ways have extended beyond her own family to the community in which she lives. Sensitive to the needs and feelings of others, she has been a helpful and generous friend, neighbour, and community member. She serves on the executive board of the West Chilcotin Museum and Historical Society, and the Community School. She is an active member of the Tatla Lake Health Society, a devoted patron of the Tatla Lake Library, a member of the book club, and is active in many other community activities. She is also a patron of the Station House Art Gallery in Williams Lake. Jen has received the Governor General's Commemorative Award for her contribution to her community and to Canada.

Loving relationships with her children and siblings; active, generous participation in her community; love of creative and performing arts; continuous learning about her country and its role in the world; all these sustain Jen King and keep her spirit young and vibrant. Her love of nature comforts and refreshes her. "When I walk in the woods," she writes, "even the trees nod a 'hello.'"

Pam Mahon

BY GLORIA ATAMANENKO

Pamela Sillar Mahon was born in 1934 in Calcutta, India, where her British-born father worked as an electrical engineer. Although she was only three-and-a-half years old when her family returned to Britain, she has many memories of Calcutta; especially the prickly heat, the lack of green spaces, and the great numbers of people. Although she learned to speak Hindustani as a little child, she no longer remembers more than a few phrases of that language.

Upon their return to Great Britain, the Sillar family rented a farm house in Argyll in western Scotland for summer use, and winters were spent in Edinburgh. During the war years, the family spent all their time in Argyll. Pam and her brother and sister loved country living. There was room to roam, animals to observe, and farm work in progress, which they tried to do. As a nine-year-old, Pam drove a team of horses at haying season. And she tried to milk an old and very patient cow. As farming country, the Argyll area is very marginal, but it produced an unusual type of food—wild rabbit meat. Gamey-tasting and unpleasant to Pam's palate, it was nonetheless a welcome source of protein during the war years. Wild rabbits were snared and their meat used by local people, and also shipped to Edinburgh.

Schooling was informal at the farm in Argyll. There was no nearby local school to

Pam Mahon arrived from England to the Cariboo after World War II with a love for animals and farming. She continues to raise cattle and sheep on her property near Miocene.

which Pam and her siblings could go, but their mother hired a retired teacher to provide education for them. She had high expectations and standards for the children, so they got a lot of homework and did not lack for learning opportunities!

"I'm just not a chicken rancher."

— PAM MAHON

In 1944, the family moved permanently to Edinburgh, with only summer holidays spent at the farm in Argyll. Going to a regular school for whole days came as a shock to Pam and her siblings, but even worse was the separation from the farm animals. Their dog and cat came with them to the city, but they were not as much fun as the horses and the cows. It felt wonderful to be back on the farm at Argyll every summer.

Summertime also brought enjoyable boating trips at sea on an old cabin cruiser that the Sillar family had bought. Pam liked being at sea, and still enjoys it, but her deeper affection is for land-based activities.

With adolescence came several years of boarding school, an experience Pam did not care for. It provided a good education, but seemed overly regimented and separated from the realities of life. After completing her studies there, she did not care to continue with more academics. She completed secretarial training but only shorthand really appealed to her (perhaps related to her artistic talent) and she can remember it to this day. A career in office work was not enticing, and "farm secretary" did not exist as a job category. She managed to get a job on a farm in Northumberland, in northern England. There she learned to drive a tractor—not as interesting a creature as a horse, but capable of producing more work faster.

Also in Northumberland, Pam met Hugh Mahon, a young man who shared her love of nature and working on the land. They married and found work near the Scottish border: Hugh as a farm foreman, and Pam was given responsibility for three cows and two hundred chickens. Her work included caring for the poultry, gathering their eggs and preparing fifty dozen of those for sale every week. "I'm just not a chicken rancher," comments Pam about that job, but it had to be done and she did it.

Pam and Hugh wanted to get a farm of their own, but buying one was prohibitively expensive, and leasing was reserved for the descendants of farmers. The Mahons did not qualify, and immigration to Canada sounded attractive and promising. Homesteading was still possible in the early 1960s, and free agricultural land seemed enticing. But they were warned that a homestead would mean life in a remote northern community, and that with two little children they might be more comfortable not to choose that option. The CPR had an immigration scheme that sounded promising. They offered good rates on a passage to Canada, with the promise of a good job and a home to live in. Ted Cornwall was the Western Agent for the CPR, and he found the Mahons a job with Hugh and Sonia Cornwall at the Onward Ranch. They worked and lived there for six years, until the Cornwalls sold the Onward, and the Mahons bought their own land.

Asked about her first impressions of the Cariboo, Pam exclaimed "Mosquitoes!" The Mahons arrived on the 1st of June, 1960. The ditches used for irrigation provided a hospitable habitat for mosquitoes, and there were swarms of them. Pam was impressed

This drawing of sheep and the drawing of the barnyard on page 150 are examples of Pam Mahon's artwork.

with the fresh, clear air, the wide expanses of land, and the forests. And she, Hugh, and their children appreciated the friendliness of Cariboo people, and the warm welcome they gave their new neighbours.

Pam is a gifted artist and delights friends with her beautiful drawings. Sonia Cornwall and her mother, Vivian Cowan, both talented artists, introduced Pam to other members of the Cariboo Art Society, and she soon became a member. Sonia and Vivian brought visiting artists to Williams Lake, and Pam took every workshop they offered. She noted with admiration that Vivian Cowan, at age sixty-five, went to the Nelson School of Art, and brought back interesting ideas and skills, and contacts. Vivian also gave art workshops to children at the Sugar Cane First Nations community. When her four children were all in school, Pam went to school also, but in a teaching capacity. She helped out with art classes and found it an enjoyable experience. "We tried out all kinds of wild and woolly projects: batik, wood sculpture, and of course, drawing."

As a member of the Cariboo Art Society, Pam also got to know people involved with the local theatre organization, and often helped to paint "backdrops" for theatrical productions. She took a workshop on pottery and was a founding member of the Cariboo Potters. Now, many years later, she is a member of the Miocene Wool Gatherers. It is a group of women who enjoy working with wool and meet to exchange ideas on spinning, weaving, and creating lovely, woolly things. Pam's attractive wool cushions are a cosy comfort.

Active participation in community organizations and countless hours of volunteer work are an integral part of Pam's life. She has served for twenty years as assistant leader of the 4H Club. "The 4H is a wonderful organization," she says. "It teaches kids poise and self-confidence, as well as good husbandry." All four of the Mahon children, Andrew, Peter, Philippa and Stephen, participated in 4H programs, and now, granddaughter Devana is involved in it as well. Pam is happy to see her so interested in animals and nature.

Pam is a director of the Miocene Community Club, which organizes many popular community events and provides space for a community preschool, and a meeting place for various community organizations. She is an active director of the Cariboo Cattlemen's Association. For many years, Pam has helped out with various aspects of the Williams Lake Stampede. She and husband Hugh provided the cattle for the "Cutting" and "Top Dog" competitions for several years. And Pam has, for a long time, played a major role in organizing the very popular "Top Dog" competition, and the less glamorous but absolutely essential clean-up phase of Williams Lake's famous yearly celebrations. Her ability to inspire others to give a helping hand, and her knack for delegating tasks are valuable talents in a community volunteer.

One of the changes Pam and Hugh had to make in coming to the Cariboo was learning the different agricultural terms used here, and skills specific to ranching. They soon blended new knowledge with what they had acquired by experience in Britain. Working on a local ranch (and Pam's twenty years of work at the Stock Yard) prepared them for developing their own Bunting Creek Ranch, which they bought in 1981. Riding to roundup cattle, branding, calving, irrigating pastures, fencing and haying, had all become familiar tasks.

Pam soon learned the value of a trained dog in managing cattle. A rancher friend gave her a scruffy-looking border collie pup whose enormous ears inspired the name Dumbo. She turned out to be an excellent helper and a loved animal friend. It was very painful to lose her when she turned fourteen. Border collies Star and Gyp are Pam's helpers now. It is fascinating to watch her communicate with them by signing and whistling. They show commendable self-restraint in manoeuvring the cattle without spooking or hurting them.

Maintaining close family relationships while living on different continents presents many difficulties. The Mahons and their families have coped well with those by telephone calls and visits. Pam loves to go back to Scotland and northern England for holidays, but she would not want to live there again. The farm in Argyll, so precious in childhood, and other rural places have been changed by increased urbanization. After the easy-going freedom of the Cariboo, the social atmosphere of Britain feels restrictive. Returning from a trip there, years ago, Pam stepped off the plane into heavy rain. But there were welcoming attendants with umbrellas to shield the arriving passengers. Pam smiled happily and thought, "This is home!"

Liz Robertson

BY KAREN LONGWELL

The best way to improve community is to become involved. This is an idea Liz Robertson made an integral part of her thirty-eight years in Williams Lake. From education to city policy to social change—Liz was a part of the community in a big way. "My theory is if you live in a community, you should make it the best you can," said Liz, an ethic her parents instilled in her at a young age. In a small city like Williams Lake, she found plenty of opportunities to do it all.

Liz was born in Keremeos, a small community in the South Okanagan, in 1932, where her family owned an orchard. She completed high school in a graduating class of five. Out of the five only two graduates, including Liz, went on to university. Liz attended the University of British Columbia for two years of an arts program and then went to what was then called Normal School to become a teacher. "This is what was expected in those days," she said. "If I'd had the chance, I would have studied to become a librarian, but UBC didn't offer a librarian program and there were no other places to study the subject in western Canada at that time."

Liz received her basic certificate and went on to teach for one year in Delta, BC, before she married Quintin Robertson, whom she had met at university. The couple had three children, two daughters and a son. The son, Ted, died in 1978. One daughter, Irene,

Liz Robertson and her husband Quint always enjoyed camping at some of the region's many rodeos. Particularly in Nemiah Valley and Anahim Lake.

lives in Victoria and Caroline lives in Brule, Alberta. They lived in North Vancouver for several years, Quintin teaching and Liz looking after the family. She worked part-time in a cooperative preschool when Caroline started school.

In 1967 Quintin felt he would like to work in a smaller school and Liz wanted a larger house so they moved to Williams Lake when Quintin got a job offer at the brand new senior secondary school—Columneezta.

Liz recalled how Williams Lake was a bit of a cow town at that time and some of the sidewalks were still wooden. After their first week in town, Liz said she was bored out of her mind and decided to get work for herself. She applied for a substitute teaching position and was hired to be Hazel Huckvale's relief teacher at Glendale Elementary School. Hazel was a well-known community advocate herself. Liz taught at Glendale for about five years and it was here she made her first mark on the community of Williams Lake. At the time there were many Punjabi students attending the school and Liz initiated the first full-time English as a Second Language program at the school. It was actually the first in Williams Lake. Liz says she really enjoyed teaching those classes. Soon there were more classes teaching young children and children's parents after school.

All the time she was teaching, Liz was also very active with the teacher's association. In 1973, Liz became the president of the Cariboo Chilcotin Teacher's Association while still teaching at Glendale Elementary School. Up until that time the job had always been done by an administrator—either a principal or vice-principal.

"I said I would be president if I could have one day off a month," Liz recalled. "It had never been done before." In that one day a month, Liz did the administrative work as president.

She was motivated to work with the association because she wanted to improve the professional development of teachers both locally and provincially. She was very proud to be a teacher and wanted to work towards the betterment of teachers and the education system. This ideal would lead to the next part of her career.

Liz gained a good reputation as elementary school teacher. She was also known in the First Nations community, having made friends in the community through teaching and travelling in the Chilcotin. With these factors in mind Liz was offered a position with UBC in 1974 to work on a new teacher trainer program in Williams Lake. The program was called the Native Indian Teacher Education Program or NITEP. It was a unique program only open to First Nations students. Students did two years work in the field and the remainder on campus. Liz said at first it was difficult to convince local teachers that it was a for-real program and students had to take the same classes as other teachers to get their Bachelor of Education. But the students from this program went on to become principals, directors of education, and basically very successful in their careers. Two graduates of the program have become leaders in education and are recognized for their contributions to the broad community. Graduate Joan Gentles is now a director of instruction with School District 27 and DeDe DeRose is an administrator in the Kamloops school system. The program was very popular and many students enrolled.

Some students did not complete the program but with a couple years of education under their belt they were able to go back to their communities and take on jobs like band councillors or education directors. Liz continued to work with the program until 1978 when she went back to teaching. She became involved in learning assistance at 150 Mile House Elementary School, which involved working with students who had trouble learning. Liz said it was a great feeling when she made a breakthrough with a student. It was very rewarding work.

"It's a great feeling to make a breakthrough with a student."

— LIZ ROBERTSON

Quintin decided to retire in 1989 and Liz thought she wasn't going to let him stay home and have all the fun so she left teaching as well. After retirement she continued to do consulting work with First Nations bands who had taken over their own schools.

Liz and Quint Robertson enjoy a casual moment together. PHOTO SAGE BIRCHWATER

In 1993 Liz ran for and was elected to city council. She served one term. She was adamant that the city should develop pride in itself. Some said businesses should show some pride but Liz said if the city doesn't set an example it's not going to happen. Through her initiative, the city council started the policy of hanging flower baskets and decorative banners. It was at this time the council organized community meetings about the housing situation. This led to SPAN (Social Planning Advisory Network) taking on the housing issue, which resulted in the Williams Lake Social Housing Society and the development of Glendale Place. SPAN is now known as the Social Planning Council of Williams Lake. Liz was one of the people who formed the organization, which looks into the social concerns and well-being of the citizens of Williams Lake. Liz enjoyed her time on council where she gained a great admiration for politicians doing "a very thankless job."

There are many people who have worked hard to develop the community, and Liz took various volunteer positions throughout her years in Williams Lake. The volunteer work she was most proud of was her involvement with the Cariboo Friendship Society where she was on the board for seventeen years. She worked on getting the present centre built and starting housing programs.

A love for art got her involved with the Station House Gallery. She wasn't one of the original members but she served as president and treasurer. Her friend Dru Hodgson, one of the orginal founders, called her one day and asked her if she would be president. This is a decision Liz never regretted. She enjoyed seeing the growth of the gallery and have it become a vital part of the community over the twenty years she was involved with the organization. Though Liz and Quint were never artists in their own right, they were always great patrons of the arts. The walls of their home were filled with the work of local artists. "Quintin and I have been pleased to support local artists," Liz would say. "My only creativity is writing grant applications."

Liz and Quintin were both rodeo fans and they volunteered countless hours working with the Stampede Association. Their forte was managing the VIP booth and they were honoured to receive lifetime passes.

The Robertsons were also very active in politics—mainly the federal Liberal Party. Both served as local federal Liberal riding association presidents at various times and they entertained cabinet ministers and senators in their home. In 1996 Liz was appointed as the returning officer for the federal riding, and was the first woman to have that position in this riding. As a returning officer she was unable to participate in politics. Although she resigned from Elections Canada in January of 2005, she continued to distance herself from any political party.

When the provincial government reorganized the health care system and created health authorities, Liz was appointed to the board of Interior Health Authority. She was also involved with SPARC BC (The Social Planning and Research Council of British Columbia). Liz always enjoyed the opportunity to work with younger people with new and innovative ideas, saying she liked to stay current on what's happening with community development issues in the province and the country.

Liz was appreciative of her husband Quintin, who was supportive of her goals and shared her interests. She said she never encountered any difficulties being a woman, and always wanted to be regarded as Liz Robertson. "The fact that I am a woman has nothing to do with it," she would say. "We liked the opportunities in Williams Lake—going to the rodeos, camping in the rural areas and getting to know such an interesting variety of people who live in the region."

Throughout their years in Williams Lake, the Robertsons talked of going back to the coast but each time they did something interesting would come up and they would want to stay. Finally in the spring of 2006 they sold their house in Williams Lake and moved to Victoria so Quint could be closer to the medical support he needed. He passed away in 2007.

Liz died a year later in the spring of 2008, at the age of seventy-six. The Station House Gallery created a park bench beside the gallery in memory of Liz and Quint who gave so much to the community, and in particular to the arts community.

Kelcy Slocombe

AUTOBIOGRAPHY

I have been a Peace Officer (Police Officer) for the Royal Canadian Mounted Police for a little over six years now and it certainly has its challenges, but also many rewards. Previously I had many other challenges which I believe played a large part in where I am today.

At the age of fifteen, I had an unexpected pregnancy, and after weighing my choices, I decided to have the baby and raise it myself. I felt at the time, with all things considered, this was the best decision for me. In retrospect, at fifteen, I don't think I really knew what I was getting myself into. The father of the baby, aged nineteen, was supportive and stuck by my decision to have the child. We both knew we were making a lifelong commitment to one another and to this unborn child. It was then several months later, at the age of sixteen, that I found myself with a newborn baby, a common-law spouse, and living in a small one-bedroom apartment in North Vancouver, British Columbia.

After getting pregnant, I attended a young parenting program at a local high school, where eventually my baby went to daycare full-time while I was in classes. As a young parent I found myself facing certain stigmas and stereotypes. For instance, that most young parents do not graduate from high school; they are on financial assistance; young parents' relationships (the mother and father of the child) do not work out; the children of young parents are less likely to be successful, etc. I found that these stigmas and stereotypes only made me more determined to prove otherwise. Regardless of the challenges that a young mother faces, I always strived for the same successes, goals and dreams that I had ever wanted.

I grew up very quickly. At a time when most teenagers were enjoying their youth, I was changing diapers, having to work extra hard at my studies, and worrying about paying the bills. I was forced to think about the life ahead for myself and for my precious child. I knew that I was determined to provide the same for my child that my parents had provided for me.

"I really wanted to make a difference in people's lives."

— KELCY SLOCOMBE

It was at the age of seventeen that I first thought about becoming a police officer. It appeared to be a very intriguing career as there was just something about it that seemed exciting and alluring. I really wanted to make a difference in people's lives and I felt that being a Peace Officer was one way that I could do this. To me, the RCMP stands for pride and it is a symbol in Canada. I knew that I wanted to be a part of this organization.

As a young woman I also thought it would be great to do something that men have not always thought a woman could, or even should, do. I grew up in a feminist era and consider myself to be somewhat a feminist. I believe in the equality of the sexes and the empowerment of women, and think this contributed to my desire to become a police officer. I felt that I would be a part of this movement in a small way.

In June of 1997 and on schedule, I graduated from high school. My plan was to get some post-secondary education under my belt and more experience in life, prior to applying to the RCMP. With this in mind I attended college for the following three years and graduated with my Associate of Arts Degree. I continued to work full-time as a clerk cashier for approximately a year and a half, then applied for and was accepted into Simon Fraser University. But rather than spend a few more years on my studies, I decided to start my application with the RCMP. It was still important for me to continue my education, but I felt that I could still do this part-time, after I got into a stable career.

The application process with the RCMP was lengthy and it wasn't until February 2003 that I started my five-and-a-half-month training at the RCMP's "Depot" Division in Regina. This was a challenging time for my family and me. My son, then seven, and my common-law spouse (the father of my child) stayed in British Columbia, while I moved away for training. It was a long haul for all of us, both mentally and physically. On July 7, 2003, I finally graduated from training and became a Peace Officer with the Royal Canadian Mounted Police. It was an incredible feeling to accomplish what I had set out to

Kelcy Slocombe beside her RCMP cruiser in Williams Lake.

do. This was in part made possible because of the huge support of my family. I was posted to "E" Division, Williams Lake, and this is where my family and I have resided since.

In August 2004, my spouse and I finally "tied the knot" (were legally married) after having been together for ten years. Since then our family has continued to grow, with two more healthy boys: one in December 2005, and our third baby in October 2008.

Being a woman doing a man's job, certainly has had its challenges, but so far, in Williams Lake, it has been a good experience. During the past two years, there have been a couple of occasions when I have felt overlooked as a female RCMP member, most likely because my physical strength and stamina were being compared to those of my peers. When referring to my peers, I am referring to the males that I work with, as the majority of other RCMP members are men. In retrospect, it is also possible that my lack of experience as a "rookie," or junior member, also played a part in these experiences. Currently, there are only five female members out of approximately fifty at the Williams Lake RCMP Detachment, but as I understand it, there are better female-to-male ratios at other detachments across "E" Division.

As a woman, doing this traditionally perceived man's job, I feel that I am constantly having to prove myself. Particularly after returning to work after a one-year maternity/paternity leave, but this may also have something to do with holding myself to such a high standard. It is also interesting to see how male police officers and female police officers operate and deal with various situations. Sometimes, there are differences that can

Dressed in red serge, Cst Kelcy Slocombe stands with her husband Jay Davis, and sons Morgan, three, and Zack, fourteen in front of the Williams Lake RCMP detachment.

be seen. For example, to see how many women opt to use their voices, compared to that of men. Not to say that males don't also use their voices, it just seems that it is used in a different manner and not as often taken advantage of. Clearly, in this day and age, it can be seen how allowing women into this workforce/career has proved an important role in the nature of police work.

Overall, the vast majority of my co-workers in Williams Lake have been great to work with and I would have to say that my workplace has a positive and friendly atmosphere. It is very clear that everyone supports one another and works cohesively to get the job done. It may very well be different at other RCMP detachments and/or at other municipal police departments, but so far, my present workplace has been quite satisfying.

As a female police officer, I am sure that I will continue to face ongoing challenges throughout the rest of my career. The only thing that I can do is to continue to do my job to the best of my ability, continue to prove those who are opposed as wrong, and continue to encourage more women to join this challenging, and yet very rewarding, career.

Cst L.K. SLOCOMBE (Kelcy)
General Duty/D.A.R.E. Officer
Williams Lake RCMP

Irene Stangoe

BY ERINN BROWN

S
he could type "like a damn," but as for composing in her own words, a young Irene Stangoe "had never thought of writing, never." Now the author of three best-selling books and hundreds of columns in the *Williams Lake Tribune* is recognized as a beloved local writer and historian.

Irene started out working as a secretary for her father's contracting business in New Westminster. As she remembers it, most women back in the thirties were starting careers as nurses or teachers. She didn't want to go into either one of them. Unsure of what she did want to do, she took her father's advice and entered into commercial courses to become a secretary and stenographer. Her life took a different turn in 1949 when she followed her husband Clive Stangoe's dream of owning a newspaper all the way up to the Cariboo.

A fellow by the name of George Renner owned the *Tribune* in the fall of that year. Were it not for a sad twist of fate, George would have passed the paper on to his son Jack. The night of the Saturday Irene visited Williams Lake, Jack Renner was coming back from Lac la Hache when the car he was riding in drove off the road. He did not survive. Left with no one to inherit the newspaper, George sold it to the people who made the first enquiry into buying it: Clive and Irene.

Shortly after she and her husband Clive Stangoe purchased the *Williams Lake Tribune,* Irene Stangoe, left, meets with Mrs. Cam Hooper, the wife of another newspaper publisher at the 1950 convention of the Canadian Weekly Newspaper Association.

Irene moved to Williams Lake with her husband early the next year. Her first impressions did not do the area justice; "Clive came up first in 1950 and it was fifty-four below Fahrenheit. I came two weeks later on the PGE and it was still forty-five below. What an introduction to the Cariboo!" The couple moved in above the old *Tribune* office on Oliver Street, beside what is currently Kondola's Furniture. Immediately when she arrived, she had to help Clive out in the *Tribune* office. She had always been a secretary, so she fell into her new role quite easily; she typed, used the linotype machine, and did a great deal of general paper pushing.

If Clive had not been so short on time as a first-time newspaper owner and editor, Irene may never have started writing. He was doing all of the running around, finding advertisers and writing stories, so he finally asked Irene to get out and cover something for him, "just out of desperation to get copy."

Her first journalistic assignment involved covering a PTA (Parent Teachers Association) meeting. As she recalls, "It was just a little PTA meeting, but I was just shaking and nervous, and I worried I was going to get something wrong."

Irene's first column started around Christmas-time in 1950, when Clive suggested that Irene visit local stores and write about what was available for Christmas. She called the column "Christmas Shopping With Irene," which was the start of the classic "With Irene" series of articles. After Christmas was over, people she knew would ask her why she didn't just keep on writing. She didn't think she had anything interesting enough to write about, but as it turned out she had enough material to last for fifty years and counting.

When she began writing her other "With Irene" articles, they were about any topic she could think of. She found a great deal of subject matter in the goings-on of her family pets, and then in stories of when her kids were born and started to grow up. Many anecdotes were told about Irene's all-time favourite pet Homer, a sweet basset hound who went everywhere with Irene. "There are still people today who say that they remember Homer. Everyone knew him."

When her editor husband didn't have time to report on something, Irene would also be the one sent to cover it. "I covered murder trials," she remembers. "Wouldn't want to do it now, I'd be too nervous. If Clive was stuck I had to go. It was something I had to do. Then I'd go home and bash it out. You couldn't sit there and think, 'Oh I could write that better. I could change it or do it some other way,' like I do now."

On another occasion, she recalls having a hard time understanding her subject matter: "Clive sent me out. They were putting the natural gas line in for the first time and something had happened. And he said you go find out what's wrong out there. So I got a hold of the main chap, one of the head men working on the line, to ask what was wrong. And he said, 'Oh well the pig blew.' And I went, now what do I ask? What's a pig? I imagined a pig exploding, like the farm animal." She laughs heartily at this point. "So I said, 'Oh yeah, mm-hmm.' The other men were standing around laughing. The main guy was trying to explain to me what a pig was, but it wasn't getting through. I finally came back to the *Tribune* and I said to Clive, 'I can't write this because I don't know what a pig is!' He didn't know either."

She also met a diverse range of people in her time at the paper. As she puts it, "The Cariboo has more than its share of...characters, I guess you'd call them." She remembers being right in the front row for everything, including Princess Margaret's visit. She also shook hands with Pierre Elliott Trudeau and met Prime Minister Mulroney when he was here. She was friends with famous Canadian author and newpaper publisher Margaret "Ma" Murray, too. Margaret used to drop in and say, "Come on, Stangoes, let's party."

Back in the days of typewriters and linotypes, when there wasn't all that much to cover in town, Irene used to write about people's personal happenings as well. One of her favourite things to cover was the weddings; "Oh the weddings...just so flowery. I used to write reams of stuff about what everybody wore and how beautiful everybody was and who presided at the urns. And I would write about the teas we used to have back when we got all gussied up with our hats and our gloves. We used to put in things about 'Oh Mr. and Mrs. Smith have gone to Vancouver for a holiday.' All that stuff."

Clive and Irene were accused at times of writing only about who the Stangoes knew. She remembers appealing for people to send information in, but they didn't, so they

Over a cup of tea in 1956, Irene Stangoe, left, interviews Pat Fulton, the wife of Cariboo MP Davie Fulton.

churned out what they knew and picked up themselves. "Lots of brick bats too, when you have a newspaper," states Irene. "Can't please everybody. Not so much myself, just the paper in general. Particularly the editor."

Anyone who's met Irene would have a hard time believing it, but she feels she can be shy and very self-conscious. "Most of my life I was essentially a very shy person," she explains. "I'll never get up and talk. I'm very nervous about that. I'd just die a thousand deaths if I had to get up and give a speech. My husband could do it at the drop of a hat. I'd often be called upon to give a toast to the men at a banquet or something and I'd be worrying about it for days, thinking, 'What am I going to say, and what if I make a mistake?' That's what I mean about being shy, being nervous about public speaking and being in the public eye. At most things, you see, I'd sit quietly in the corner and record things and then I'd just have to go back and write it."

She wrote her "With Irene" column until 1962, but with the paper getting bigger and her kids getting old enough to become embarrassed by Irene writing about them, she knew it was time to retire the column. She might have stopped writing altogether right then. Instead she switched gears and, after retirement in 1975, started writing an historical column, "Looking Back", about bygone days in the Cariboo Chilcotin. Many of those columns along with other stories Irene gathered were published in three books: *Cariboo Chilcotin Pioneer People and Places* (1994); *Looking Back at the Cariboo Chilcotin* (1997); and *History and Happenings in the Cariboo Chilcotin* (2000).

Irene is humble about her accomplishments, which may be one of the reasons she's earned the respect of so many in her lifetime. "I don't know whether I had any knack for it or not. I didn't just go in and say 'Ooookay now.' Y'know?" she laughs. "You just admire something around the kitchen or try to get at ease with the people. I guess you just develop your own pattern and way of doing it."

She says she wasn't aware she was doing all those things but looking back, she can see it now. "I talk about being shy now, but I don't remember being shy at the time. I remember being nervous going down the corridor to the PTA meeting, but after a while I didn't give it much thought."

Irene says she doesn't consider herself a pioneer in the newspaper field because there were lots of other women writing. "I was saying to Clive though, there were just the two of us for the longest time covering things. I can't remember when we started getting reporters to come in. I had our daughter Elaine in 1951, so I wasn't able to be down there running out to meetings like I did before. We must have started getting some people soon after that."

Reflecting back, Irene says it has really been a wonderful life. "When I think back on it, it's been exciting, fun. I've often said that the only reason I got into writing was because I was married to the editor; I had to. I had never thought of writing, never. If anyone had told me back then that I would still be writing for the *Tribune* fifty-odd years later, or that I would have three books published, I would have thought they were crazy. Back then we had typewriters and linotypes, no computers."

Coping

PERSONAL ADVERSITIES AND FINDING STRENGTH

Linda-Lou Howarth

DEALING WITH A STROKE

I climbed out of the tub and felt sick to my stomach. My head felt very light, so I decided to lie down for a few minutes like I always did after a hot bath. As I walked to the bed I was staggering to the left. My face felt like someone was dragging their hand down the left side pulling my skin downward. My left arm felt like it was being pulled too and my brain felt as though it was being short-circuited. Wondering what the heck was going on I got up to get dressed, and fell to the left, bumping into the wall. Crap! I landed on the bed again and my face was really being pulled.

Yikes! What the heck is going on? My face on the left side was really sagging. Man, I must be having a stroke. How can that be? I am only forty-seven years old. I flew off the bed and into my jogging pants and T-shirt and started down the hall, bumping into the walls as I walked. I made it outside to yell at Evan to come help. He hurried over and I told him what happened. He said he best get me to the hospital.

I had the stroke on March 17, 1999, and spent one month in hospital in Kamloops. I felt like a kid in the recovery program there, and just did what they asked. I cried when my family left to go home, and I worked well with the rehab staff, but never understood what happened to me.

One month later I came home, and lived in a wheelchair. I would go to bed and my daughter, Shelly, who was still at home, would cut up a big bowl of fruit for me. After I struggled out of bed in the morning, I would wash up, get dressed and sit in the wheel-chair watching TV and eating the fruit from 8 a.m. until noon. It was the loneliest time of my life because hardly any of my friends called or came to visit. It was like I didn't exist anymore. I cried a lot but tried not to let my family know. Apparently crying and depression are all part of the stroke, as well as laughing wildly at the stupidest things.

I decided I was not going to be a wheelchair person and within a month I returned it. Before I got rid of the wheelchair, my family bought me a little toy poodle terrier cross I called Alice. She is very smart and my best buddy.

I learned to cope with my problems and do the morning dishes. I could wash the plates no problem, but doing the silverware was hard. I couldn't hold them in my left hand, so I draped the wash cloth over the edge of the sink and ran the silverware along the cloth to get them clean.

After I mastered the dishwashing, I started to sweep the floor. A lady came out to clean the house, change the sheets, dust, and do the laundry, but it wasn't long before I told her not to bother coming out anymore. Shelly would keep the house fairly clean when she came home from work, and I decided that my therapy would be to do the dishes and sweep the floors. It was very time consuming, but it helped to pass the time.

My next goal was to make the bed. Progress was slow but time flew. Each day I would work at keeping the house tidy and work on getting more use out of my arm and make my leg and foot work. The doctor prescribed a foot brace, which I used for a bit, but then decided how the heck can I make my foot work if it is clamped in a brace. So it was tucked into a drawer and I concentrated on making sure my foot went the right way, no slacking off.

I would get mad at my arm as it would clam up and not do what I wanted it to do. I repeatedly hit it with my right hand until it would relax, all the while yelling at it to smarten up. Again my girls and Evan would laugh at me until I would burst into giggles. If I was holding something in my left hand, I could not loosen my grip, so everyone made a game of yanking it out of my hands. Again I would double over in peals of laughter.

Near the middle of May I began to go for walks. At first only about a hundred yards, but by the end of two weeks I was walking quite a ways. With Alice bouncing alongside me making me laugh, I took in the sunshine, the bright blue skies, the birds, and enjoyed the freedom to move. Not very fast, but I moved regardless.

I was enjoying life without the pressure of before. Progress. At one point I got a brain wave of going for a bike ride, so I wheeled the bike out on the road and climbed on. I gave a shove but before I could get it going I lost my balance and landed with a bang on the left side. I crawled slowly to my feet, put the bike away, and then sat down and wallowed in my pain as I had banged my head. Guess I won't be riding a bike again for awhile. No wonder everybody always says, "Linda-Lou!" in that tone of voice. I sure earned it at that moment.

I went from the wheelchair to the four-pronged cane, to the single cane, all in two months. Never once did I look back and wish I had done such and such. I felt grateful that I survived the stroke as successfully as I had. Grateful that I was alive, grateful that I could make progress on getting my nimbleness back, such as it used to be.

I did get a bit depressed. I went to the doctor, who prescribed pills. After two days I threw them out because my cure did not only involve me, it involved my husband as well.

The support from my family was awesome. They always say: "Linda-Lou!" in a horrified voice if I do something they think is too dangerous. Like climbing up on a chair to put the curtains back up. I'd just laugh; no big deal. It is a step forward for

On May 22, 1999, Linda-Lou Howarth gets into the saddle for the first time after her stroke with the help from daughter, Shelly.

me to accomplish the little things each day. One thing with the stroke was learning to ask for help. I always had trouble keeping up with the rest of the family before the stroke. But afterwards I didn't even try to keep up with Evan or the girls. They constantly forgot that I could not keep up with them, "just jump up and roar off." They'd be half a mile away while I was just managing to get out of my chair. They were always in a hurry, everything just had to be done on the run. So after the stroke they really had to slow down if they wanted to keep an eye on me. I would be slowly walking along and Evan would say, "Hurry up! Run!" I would tell him, "I am! Can't you tell?" Then I would have to stop because I was laughing so hard I couldn't keep my balance.

One of the hazards of a stroke is choking. Just out of the blue I'd start to choke. My family could only sit and watch and make sure I had water to drink. I'd be sound asleep and wake up choking. Evan soon learned not to sleep with his arm around me, because I would almost panic trying to get a decent breath.

In May of 1999, Evan was holding his horse-training clinic and I got on my horse, Sister, and went for a ride. I couldn't get on gracefully but I got on. We went for an hour-long ride, which in my world at the time, was forty-five minutes too long, because I could not use my left leg to cue Sister, who started to jig. This would hurt my arm because it would flop loosely up and down. But then I would giggle at the humour of my arm flopping up and down uselessly. It is hard to be angry and laugh at the same time. I was angry because I could not stop Sister from jigging downhill. That was awful.

This gelding thoroughly enjoys a neck massage as Linda-Lou demonstrates techniques learned at the College of Equine Therapy.

In May we started branding. I couldn't just sit there so I placed the tags in the tagger and handed them to the person doing the tagging. I'd take the empty tagger and fill it. At least I felt useful.

By June 1999 I was back to driving my truck, a standard. At first I made sure Melodie, our oldest, was with me to take over because I easily got tired.

August came, and I had the camper put on, and went to the family reunion. Just me and Alice. One night we were all sitting around the campfire listening to the guys sing and play guitar, and a big windstorm came up and the rain came pelting down. Everyone jumped and grabbed their chairs and ran to the shelter. So I did too. In slow-motion. I got out of my chair, grabbed my umbrella; everyone was all cozy under cover already. The wind came whipping around, grabbed my umbrella, and away I went, no control. I had no balance, and was going with the wind.

In the fall I went on the roundup a few times. I had to use a stump or a big rock to get on my horse, but I climbed on Sister and she and I rounded up three hundred head all by ourselves.

As I got steadier on my feet I would stomp around in the living room, doing my version of dancing. By 2000 I was able to do a slow dance at the New Year's Dance. By 2005 I could polka with the best of them and not even get winded.

The doctor told me that I would only have minimal recovery and my first thought was I won't be able to dance. Then the next thought was, oh yes I will. I worked at the dancing in the living room with Alice watching.

In June of 2000, I substituted as the secretary at the Riske Creek School for a couple of weeks. I was the secretary there before the stroke. So I filled in and really enjoyed that.

In May 2000 I was determined to help in the branding. I managed to stick it out for a little while then would power out and rest a bit. The guys would cover for me, then when I was ready they would move over to allow me to brand again. My job was to do the actual branding of the calves.

I cannot sit around for too long, my back gets sore, so I went outside and clambered around until I got in the flower beds and began to pull weeds. It wasn't long before I heard

"Linda-Lou! What are you doing?"

"I'm doing therapy," was my reply. After being warned to be careful, the ever-watchful daughters or husband would go in the house, but I could feel them checking on me every once in a while. My flower beds looked good that year.

I did spend a bit of time on the Internet, talking to others who had strokes but I found it too gloomy. Too sad. Everyone dwelt on their problems and were not trying to make themselves better. So I told everybody goodbye and signed off.

That year I got my hands on an older-model sewing machine, and began to sew up cowboy scarves which I sold to the cowboys at cow camp. I made a pretty good job of selling them. For Christmas I made shirts for the guys in our daughters' lives. One son-in-law and two prospective sons-in-law, and shirts for my husband Evan. I even sewed myself a pair of pants.

I got the call from the BC College of Equine Therapy that they were accepting me to take their twenty-month course. So in March 1999 Melodie and I went to check it out. Year 2000 saw me in college learning all about horses and their anatomy. I began in September, and travelled down once a month to Vernon and stayed for two days at a time. There were twenty in our class. People helped me only if they thought I needed it.

Each month I headed home to work on twenty or more horses. Each and every horse really appreciated a massage. While I managed to pass the program, though not with flying colours, I can still help a horse out of a lot of problems.

In October I started to cook for the cowboys at Fosberry cow camp. That is an awesome job. I had horses galore to massage, time to study, and cooking in a cool cabin. Our daughter Racquel was one of the hands there, with her husband Ed. Racquel would get up early with the rest of the guys, saddle her horse, eat and leave. Then come home, tend to her horse, the dogs, and then dash in to see what kind of help I needed. Then she would wash the dishes for me.

I hit the books in the mornings after cleaning up the breakfast mess. Then I'd go out and massage a couple of horses, then spend the afternoon baking bread, cookies, cakes, cinnamon buns and dinner buns for the cowboys to munch on. Their compliments let me know I had done good.

While in college I stayed with good friends, Minnie and Earl Hawthorne, in Salmon Arm, just half an hour from Vernon. I was whining that I had trouble peeling potatoes and carrots, and buttering toast, and Earl disappeared and came back in with a small board that had two nails about an inch apart poking through. "What's that for Earl?" I asked. "Well," he says, "It's like this. You jab the potato on the nails, then you can peel them with no trouble."

Then Earl whipped out another board with three sides on it. "This is for you to put your toast in, to butter it." I gave Earl a big hug.

In 2003 JoAnn Hamm introduced me to FlyLady.net, a website that helps everyone keep their places spotless, using routines and working fifteen minutes at a time. Now I am proud of my house and no longer stress over it being messy because in fifteen minutes it can be presentable.

In 2003 I attended college to take the Applied Computing course to update my knowledge so I could find a job. It was in computer class that I discovered I could type just as fast as the teacher could talk.

I never worry about being able to use just one hand. I often think that when my girls were small I already practised using one hand. While packing them I'd have to use one hand to hold them and work with the other.

I spent the full year of 2004 typing out resumés, handing them out, and hoping for an awesome job. But no such luck. Nobody wanted me. Now I was beginning to feel sorry for myself. At times I would be made aware that I was handicapped, even though I didn't feel handicapped. I mentioned this fact to friends and they told me that they didn't even think of me as being handicapped. That was nice. At one time I had the "handicap" parking sign for my truck. I think I may have used it two times, then I lost it, and never ordered another one. I figured if I parked close, how could I get my therapy by walking only a few feet.

I have been working hard at getting better. I take my blood pressure pills, I signed up to Sun Rider to use their foods, which really help my body and muscles. I make sure I get a massage at least once a month, and I exercise and keep totally aware of what my body is up to.

When I first had the stroke, the left side of my face was relaxed but by the time I got to Kamloops, God must have decided to make the muscles work properly because my face is fine now. Only when I get really tired does my left side relax a bit, my mouth droops a bit, and my left eye droops too. I can walk almost normally now, as I worked hard at being aware of which muscles are not doing their job; I massage them or have someone do it for me.

In the years since my stroke I've come a long way. I am still going to improve more. Nothing will hold me back; I am always trying new things, or figuring out ways to do something.

Before the stroke Evan bought me a guitar that I plunked away on. George Strait wouldn't be calling me up as a backup singer, but I could strum away and wail to my heart's content when by myself. I miss playing, and it is the nicest-sounding guitar ever. But, hey, I just may play it again one day.

On May 3, 2005, our daughter Racquel, and her husband Ed Russell brought a baby boy into this world. One more reason to really work towards improving my health. I want to spend time with him, watch him grow, show him how to do a thing or two. Kagen Dally Russell is the best inspiration ever.

Sheila Gruenwald

AUTOBIOGRAPHY

As I clenched my degree and held it high for the world to see, the wind embraced and acknowledged my victory. Flooding like a torrent, the memories surged past my eyes in hot tears of passion. Fleeting before me were the memories of each step it took to be here today. The painful and the joyful, each responsible for moulding me into the woman of courage that I am today.

Long had I held onto the belief that it was my choice to let life's adversities develop the character within me or to crumble in their wake. Each time life had slapped me down I chose to stand up more full of character than before. My heart began to race as my life unfolded before me. Suddenly I was there standing before my mother.

"I am not lying, I am telling the truth," I pleaded emphatically, brushing the hot tears from my dirty face into my hair. In all my ten years I had never been more terrified. "Don't you make up such lies about people. Go to your room!" my mother berated me.

As I quietly obeyed I played back the vision in my head of what had just happened. We were just playing, like we often did, building mud castles, chasing frogs and crawling through culverts. But that is where it all changed. How did it happen? Right, he asked me to wait for him, that he had something to show me. As he crawled up beside me I knew something was wrong but it was too late to move, we were too far into the culvert. He started to touch me. When I told him to stop he began to kiss me so I couldn't talk. Why was he doing this to me? I tried to push him away but there was no space to move. Suddenly I was terrified and could not understand why this was happening. I don't remember how long it was, I just knew it was wrong.

Then he was gone. I gathered myself together and began to crawl out of the culvert. When I reached the end a foot came towards my face. It was him again. "Don't you tell anybody, you hear me?" He threw a rock at my face. "If you plan on telling I won't let you out of this culvert." He kicked at me again.

Unwillingly, I promised not to tell, knowing full well I would as soon as I got home. As I lay there I heard his footsteps retreat towards home, my home, where he was a guest.

Uncertain of the time passed, I cautiously crawled to the road above and made my way sheepishly home. How would I tell my mother? We never had a very close relationship but I knew I could count on her in a time like this.

Suddenly the door slammed and brought me back to the present. Standing there with anger beyond my understanding was my mother, willow switch in hand. "How can you make up such lies about people? You are grounded for six months. Now get over here." As she pulled me over her lap for my spanking, my respect for her dissipated and anger swelled to the point of wanting vicious retaliation.

The next day I could not and would not look at my mother. I felt a deep void that at this time would remain empty. Slowly as the days passed into months I became angrier. My dad, a former Armed Guard for the United States Army, began to train me in his art. The art that had no name but full of purpose: to disarm and kill the opponent. Within this art my anger surged to the top. A revengeful desire welled up inside of me—now I could get even. Now was the time I could get back what had been stolen from me. Soon my skill surpassed my age and my temper surged beyond control, beyond my father's control. He refused to teach me anymore. He was afraid of who I had become. Determined not to loose this opportunity to gain back my dignity, I chose to keep training, in secret, from memory and from books.

I began to fight everyone and everything, adding to my roster of classmates sent to the hospital. The temporary satisfaction this provided was not enough to fill the void within. Now months passed into years and I segregated myself from my peers with lewd and obnoxious comments and behaviours. My heart yearned for friendships that I could not hold. I gravitated towards the male population because I could be cool with them. They could take my physical and mental militant stance towards the world.

At fifteen I found true love with a fellow who promised to be with me forever. A month before my sixteenth birthday I gave him the only part of me I had left, my virginity. We grew together and faced many storms but my fears and insecurities crushed him.

Sheila Gruenwald is realizing her strength after enduring a lengthy abusive relationship. She has written a book about her experiences and gives workshops to other women faced with abusive relationships.

His support was endless. He helped me to leave my house and become established on my own when I was a mere sixteen years old. But there was something else burning inside of me that could not be named or filled. Feeling a deep need to be challenged, almost contained, I broke the relationship eighteen months later.

My life had become fast-paced. I hid in a flurry of activities and self-imposed commitments. I worked two jobs, attended school full-time, participated on sports teams and maintained my own home. I began to date erratically, drink freely and give myself freely to men. That void was getting deeper and more defined in my life.

It was a cool, crisp January when the question came that was to change my life as I could have never imagined.

As he casually put his fingers in his jean pocket he looked me in the eye and nodded his head towards my hand. "So, when did you break up with your boyfriend?" It took me a moment to understand what he was talking about.

"Oh, you mean the ring. That is nothing. My sister and her husband bought that for me when I was twelve. I have it at home being cleaned."

His stature straightened as he poised himself for his next inquiry. "Would you like to go to the movies with me tonight?"

I paused and waited, never before had I dated an East Indian. He seemed to be so real and gentle, so I agreed.

Clean-shaven, leather jacket, tight jeans and polished Datons, he came to pick me up. His demeanour was gentle but strong. He terrified me yet set me at peace like no one else ever had. We chose to see *Witness* that night; the unknown heartbeat of a relationship yet to come.

Perplexed by his intrigue and flattered by his doting I agreed to go out with him again a few days later. He had been drinking when he picked me up but it didn't bother me. We went for a drive and sat in the serenity of the night talking. He then took me for a longer drive into the remote surrounding area. As he parked the car I could feel a difference in the air. Looking through me with eyes of contention he told me to "put out or get out." Armed with the fury of my childhood and the knowledge learned from my dad, I told him he would be driving me home. Seemingly defeated by my strength he started the car and drove me home.

> *"I am a woman of courage and I will succeed."*
>
> — SHEILA GRUENWALD

Many days passed before I would take his calls again. When I did he was greatly apologetic and appealed for my forgiveness. Longing for the strength he offered I relinquished my position and agreed to go out with him again. He continued to show his affection and showered me with gifts and signs of admiration. Missing my fast-paced past I gave myself to him in a hotel room.

The next morning I was devastated that once again I had let myself down. My tears spoke to his heart and he embraced me with warmth and understanding. At that moment we both fell in love. Our relationship continued to grow and I felt a desire to please him like no other. Security was creeping into my heart and peace was begging to bud. Yet there was an untold surprise still to unfold.

Hot tears pouring down his face, he came to my door. We went for a drive through town and parked in front of a local park. There he told me he was on his way to Vancouver to pick up his wife. Caught in a torrent of emotions cast between despair, anger and understanding, I bravely relinquished my position as his girlfriend and freed him to fulfill his obligations.

Many weeks passed without seeing him and things began to smooth out again when he strode back into my life. He confessed his love for me could not be forgotten and asked if we could continue the relationship. He assured me that his marriage was over. Longing for the strength he provided I accepted his offer and began dating him again. Soon we were living together and making plans for our future. At the youthful age of eighteen we pledged ourselves to one another. At nineteen I was pregnant with our first child.

In an attempt to separate myself from my childhood pains we made a move to Surrey, a move from which I would learn many life's lessons. As we forged ahead together we faced many of the challenges that young couples face. It wasn't until four years later that the trials we faced became distinctive from other couples. He began to drink. We began to fight. Our marriage began to fall apart.

The fights began as yelling matches that soon turned into physical contests, most of which I lost. At this point in my life I had relinquished my desire for fist fights for the joy of motherhood: a joy that was slowly being stolen away. By this time we had two children and a growing trucking company. Our desire to stay together was strong but so were our wills. At twenty-four I was pregnant with our third child but soon lost it.

Accused of aborting it, I had a deep desire to show him that it was truly a miscarriage so I became pregnant again. This pregnancy turned out to be a physical and mental trial. My blood pressure began to drop as well as my energy. I struggled to take care of our two children and our business. The tension began to rise and in a fit of anger he wrapped his hands around my neck and strangled me to the point just before passing out. I only remember begging for the unborn child's life and the look back at me that was completely void. The abuse was out of control and I pulled further and further away from him. I pressed charges and secured a restraining order but it didn't keep him away. He watched me from the bushes that surrounded my house. I was terrified.

With an apparent change of heart he came back to me. He promised to never hurt me again and to begin counselling. Longing for my life to be normal I accepted him back into the house. I even went before the judge and dropped the charges. Life in our house was serene and peaceful as we welcomed our daughter into the world. The tempo began to slowly change and I turned into the security of my children; knowing they needed me, I found strength to continue. At this point I realized there could be no prolonged peace in the house. I began to prepare myself mentally to leave him. The abuse heightened to the point where he raped me and I became pregnant yet again.

Upon return from the confirming doctor's appointment I packed the camper and my children and headed home to Williams Lake. My original intention was to give him a shock so that he would realize what he was sacrificing. To my chagrin a female voice began to answer his phone eight days after his children and I left him.

Devoid of all understanding I buried myself in my children. I was mindful to raise my boys knowing that abuse was not the way to treat a woman, and to raise my girl knowing it was not okay to be treated that way. I committed myself to give my children every tool and all the awareness they would need to be honourable citizens. Three young children aged eighteen months, four years and six years old and pregnant with the fourth, I soon found myself emotionally and physically exhausted. Fantasies of revenge began to fill my nights. "How could he turn his back on his own flesh and blood?"

Dangerously close to a complete breakdown, my mind entertained morbid thoughts of levelling the score. The void in my life was now filled with hatred so poisonous I was willing to sacrifice my own standard of living to satisfy it. The only sane thought I had was that of my children. "What would they do if I killed their father and I was in prison?" They would be subject to foster care all of their lives. It was a price I was not willing to let them pay for their father's transgressions. This was neither the first nor the last time that the focus on my children kept me honest, alive or sane.

Challenges continued to present themselves through the winter as I adjusted to being single and on welfare. I had to learn to budget all of my expenses for less than what I was accustomed to investing each month. Many times I thought of going back, afraid I would never be able to provide for my children financially like their father could. I began to read the Bible and attend church. Slowly I gained back some of my strength but I still could not see the world objectively. My opinions where strongly subjective to my past and I continued to keep people pushed away.

The end of January saw the birth of my son. I still see the people there supporting me... none of whom was his father. Three weeks after his birth I apologized to him for all of the horrible thoughts I had about him and his father while I was carrying him. He waved his hand at me and a tear came from his right eye. A true sign of forgiveness as babies' tear ducts are not yet formed at three weeks old. At that time the Lord gave me a song for him. I could not understand it but it brought me and my baby peace and strength.

The birth of a son brought his father around. Again he pleaded with me and promised me he had changed. He confessed that he had treated me very poorly but he had been sober for over three months. We began talking on the phone and soon he moved to Williams Lake and was living with his family again. With counselling and a renewed desire to make our marriage work we forged ahead yet again. Our marriage was as close to perfect as it had ever been: honest and open communication and a renewed passion and compassion for the future. We bought a home together and moved in on our oldest son's birthday.

As much as I desired a future with this man I could not let go of the past. I could not let go of the pain he had willfully inflicted on me. And even the children. Not paying child support and stealing our vehicle in the middle of the night. I no longer knew this man. I could not trust him as much as I wanted to. Soon my unbelief in him could not be contained within the confines of my mind, it began to show. Feelings of insecurity welled up inside of him and he began to drink again. Then the abuse started again. Being more aware, I acted immediately and made him leave.

Determined to be independent I chose to work an hour and a half out of town as a P.E. teacher. The hours were long and demanding but the pay was good enough that I could make it working only two days. I worked sixteen hours a day on Tuesdays and

Thursdays; the rest of the week was filled with caring for my four children and the home. I also owned and operated a gymnastics club on Saturdays. Seven months of running this schedule and I was beginning to burn out physically. I was falling asleep driving and almost died twice. Then the ultimate price was paid. Leaving a burner on by accident my home was burned to the ground on Mother's Day 1998. Following was a horrible time of accusations, paperwork and dishonourable dealings by those whom I counted on to deal fairly. My emotional, physical and spiritual strength faced the ultimate tests. Though I had left the church I was attending, many of the people rallied around me and gave me strength that I did not have. Again the void in my life was being filled with the love of God though I was too blind to see it.

A father of one of my gymnastics students gave me his fully furnished trailer to live in. Strangers knocked on church doors to find me and bless me with much-needed clothing and food. People I barely knew brought me money and food. It was amazing! My faith in human kind was being restored.

A tear rolls down my cheek as I hear my pastor's voice. "Pete is dead. This is what you need to do…" His voice continued on and I was taking notes. He was telling me which plane I needed to get on to get home. How can this all be happening? Here I am at school in Victoria trying to get my master's degree. For the second year in a row a tragedy has tried to take my focus. On Wednesday of this week I had received a call telling me that one of my students had been killed. And now today it was the father of my children. I was numb. Hanging up the phone, I walked across the dorm hall and told a dear friend what happened. My knees collapsed and my stomach turned as guilt set in. For so long I had wanted him dead, to quit stalking me, to quit hurting me, to quit neglecting his children…and now it happened. Had God really listened to me? What had I done?

Then I remembered the warning dreams my pastor's wife had, my sister had, and that I also had. I told him and he knew, but he didn't change. And now it happened, he was gone. Swallowed into the depths of the lake in a drunken soirée. How sobering his last moments must have been. Friends told me that he had surfaced twice and on his last time he had called out the name of Jesus. "All those who call upon my name will be saved." At least I know he is in Heaven, that his pain is gone and that he can now come to peace with the memories that taunted him and caused so much anxiety in our marriage.

I hated him for being in Heaven and leaving me to fill the gap of father, mother, breadwinner, and the list goes on. And then I came to the realization that God is now my husband and my children's father. He is my provider and comforter. God has been faithful in providing for me. In desperation I had cried out for security in my life. A matter of weeks later found me in my own home. A single mother with four children, a student with temporary employment, I was able to secure financing on a home and my children and I moved in.

God has also made it possible for me to stay at home and home-school my children.

I have a phenomenal source of income and am able to do the things I love. I have also become a foster parent to a young man labelled as high risk. He has been a great blessing to our home as well as providing some great growing opportunities. The void I have felt for so many years has been filled with love and now I am able to love. It took the children in my life, my own and the ones I have worked with over the years, to teach me how to love unconditionally. As an adult I have come to know sustained relationships. I have a deep compassion for those who have been wounded by the tides of life and seek opportunities to encourage them and to listen to their stories.

In all of this I have found the time to complete my master's degree in Leadership and Training. My research project dealt with accelerating academic achievement in underachieving youth. And now I will forge ahead, helping those children who have difficult times learning, and those who have been cast to the side. I will share their pain, encourage their dreams and validate their goals. If I can help one child to achieve their goals then the trials and tribulations I have faced will not have been in vain.

As I pull my degree to my chest, I turn and walk off the podium, knowing I am a woman of courage and I will succeed.

Heather Fraser

HOPES & DREAMS OF A BETTER LIFE

Did you ever try too hard that you were destined to fail; no matter what you did, it was never enough; you could never possibly live up to the many expectations of you? That's the story of my life. The telling of it hurts unendingly. Looking back, it may not have been such a bad thing. I got away with a lot, simply because I was expected to screw up. It was always: "There she goes again!" or "What is she up to now?" I did get away with a lot because of it, and in some ways I'm proud of that. I tried for a lot of years to be what was expected of me, but in doing so, I wasn't being true to myself. I tried to live up to images I knew weren't real, only to end up miserable and hating myself.

My life should have been simple and easy, but it wasn't. My first memory is of pain, and I learned first-hand the meaning of desperation and lack of control of even the simplest things in life. I was loved; I know that. I was raised by very strong, independent women; my great-grandmother and two aunts. They were beautiful women in every aspect of the word. How I admired them, and how short our time together seems. They carry me through this life.

My mom and dad separated when I was just over a year old. Both equally abusive to the other, I grew up on stories of the fights they had. When they did talk about "her" it was always in a derogatory way. She was someone not spoken of, or it would lead to one heck of a rough night. I met my mom later in life, and now I know why.

At one-and-a-half years of age, my sister and I moved back to my dad's hometown so my aunt could take care of us while Dad worked away from home. That was the beginning of some of the best and worst times of my life. When Dad was away it was the best of times. When he was home, it was the worst of times. No one ever knew what would set him off. When Dad was drinking, you just knew a fight would eventually happen. He would bring friends home from the bar just to have someone to fight with, and if that didn't work, there was always someone at home to beat.

My first memory is of pain, and I'm sure it will be my last. He beat anyone in his way when the mood hit him. The only one that was safe was my great-grandmother. She was spared the physical abuse but saw what he put on everyone. The one who suffered most was my aunt, who became Mommy to my sister and me.

The gist of it was that we were a loving and caring family when Dad wasn't around. When he was there, it was a different story. He beat Mommy and her husband on a regular basis until her husband finally left her. Charlie couldn't handle the abuse for very long and thankfully he went on to lead a good life away from it all as much as possible. What it did to Mommy though, I can only guess. He was supposed to be her husband and protector, but abandoned her to the rest of her life. Nothing but abuse. I saw her pain but only now understand it.

Once Charlie left, the abuse got worse, if that's possible. Mommy's sunglasses were a regular accessory of hers after the beatings. She always walked and moved slowly from the pain of the beatings she took.

Life was really just beginning for me, but I had already known and had seen too much. The worst was yet to come. I always was a chatty child with no secrets around me. It really got bad though for me when one of Mommy's boyfriends "touched" me and I said so at the dinner table. The memory is burned into my brain for all time. The beatings that ensued that day are forever etched in my memory. It has made me who I am today. Dad heard it and I have not seen to this day, anyone beaten so badly in my life. Needless to say, that boyfriend didn't stay around much longer. And when he was around, beatings were on a regular basis; even still he came back a few years later.

Another boyfriend came around, along with more "touching." As always, I spoke my mind. As always, more beatings ensued. This happened from the age of three to roughly six years old. It seemed that with every boyfriend Mommy had it was the same thing. I know what it did to me, but I can only imagine what it did to her. In the end, no boyfriends for her, only abuse when Dad was home for her "letting" it happen.

We loved each other so hard when Dad was away and tried to protect each other when he was home. Early on it was always as though I was the older sister. I would jump up and say or do anything I could think of to distract Dad from the abuse he gave out so easily. It seemed sometimes that he had more patience for me, so a song and dance or a smile could distract him. If not, I threw myself into the middle of the fray with no thought for myself, only wanting it to stop. Something changed though, and I'm not sure what it was or when it happened.

I was nine or ten when things changed. Dad had been my protector of sorts even through the other abuses, but suddenly all that ended. It seemed innocent at first. "Oops Dad, I'm sorry, I didn't know you were in the bathroom." Then it went to him calling me into the bedroom or bathroom when he was undressed. I remember covering my eyes, but at the same time being curious about our differences. I curse myself for that curiosity every day because it led again to the "touching." Again I told whoever would listen, but it was different this time. Dad didn't come rushing in to "save" me. He was the abuser, and there was no knight in shining armour to save me from it all.

> ## "I always told, but no one listened."
>
> — HEATHER FRASER

It went on for years. An eternity it seemed. Dad would make excuses to friends and family to be alone with me. I made it worse because I cried and would wet myself trying to get away. But then, who wanted to be around me if I was such a pain in the ass? Who knew when I would break out in a fit and embarrass someone? No one wanted to take me anywhere, so I was left to Dad to "deal with." And deal with me he did, just like he did to Mommy. We each paid a high price and still do.

I always told, but no one listened. He was well-known to everyone, even with the abuse he gave. Somehow he was still respected, or maybe he was feared.

He stopped abusing me only when I moved out at the age of sixteen. I met a guy and got pregnant. He knew the abuses I took and was going to save me from it all. The relationship ended before I knew I was pregnant, but I still held out high hopes of him saving me when I told him. It didn't happen that way though. My dreams of two-and-a-half kids, white picket fence and a home were gone in an instant. I remember Dad trying the "shot gun" wedding type thing, and I ran away from home. It was my first real taste of courage and rebellion. No one was going to save me but me. It turns out that he never even knew.

I ran away to the city to an unwed mothers' home, lost, scared to hell, and not knowing which way was up. The counsellors there gave me more backbone, and the first real sense that what I thought was a normal life, wasn't at all. I stood up to Dad for the first time in my life, but in doing so I became an outcast.

My dad passed away in 2004. People ask why, if he's done so much to me, do I still love and talk to him. I just do. "How can you forgive him?" they say. I didn't. I just knew that to hate him would hurt me more than it did him.

I was called to see my dad. He was sick from a stroke, and I knew he was dying. He asked for me and I went to him without thought. He was waiting for me. True to form Dad put a sexual innuendo on my putting lotion on his legs. He said to me, "Heather, I think you like that." That one phrase, those few words killed me in every way possible. I left him and came back home the next day, where I lost my mind.

Dad took a turn for the worse the next day and my sister called me, begging me to come back even though I tried to explain what had happened. Tried to explain how I just couldn't. I had already done and said all I could, to no avail.

I pray every night for some sense of understanding, some meaning to this life I lead. There seems to be none. So I still go on, still hope, still dream.

I can write and say this now because everyone is gone. There is no one left to hurt but me. What they never knew is that I didn't set out to hurt anyone. I just said what needed to be said. My Mommy died when I was eleven. He beat her to death on top of the drinking which she did to herself. Her courage lives on in me though, as well as her hopes and dreams of a better life.

The only thing I can add is that I did go back home before my father passed away. At that point he could not speak because of numerous strokes he had had. I stayed with him until his last breath, and I can only say that he spoke volumes with his eyes, apologizing in his own way for all the years of abuse. I had not wanted to go back, but it was the most powerful experience of my life and I would never change that. I held his hand and let him and all our grief slip away with him.

Debra McNie

AUTOBIOGRAPHY

*I*f life is considered a journey, my life took an unexpected detour down a path of chronic illness and toward one of discovery, acceptance and change. Before becoming ill, I considered myself a high-functioning woman able to keep up with the demands of motherhood, marriage and a career. I was teaching dance and working full-time, when illness, like a blanket of mysterious mist, engulfed my life. For a time darkness fell upon me.

Chronic illness can range from fibromyalgia, lupus, arthritis, hepatitis, multiple sclerosis, chronic fatigue, to many others. I have been diagnosed with fibromyalgia and chronic fatigue and a rare immune deficiency disorder called C2 (Complementary 2) deficiency. Missing the C2 gene prevents my immune system from receiving the correct messages to effectively fight infections. C2 symptoms are similar to those of lupus. I experience severe muscle and joint pains, fatigue, insomnia, nausea, headaches, brain fog and at times depression. Often I am hospitalized due to an autoimmune response, which causes my immune system to attack major organs, such as my heart and kidneys. At times my greatest challenge is just to get out of bed, or go to bed, depending on whether I am experiencing fatigue or insomnia.

When I first became seriously ill, I had no idea I would still be fighting this battle five years later (now sixteen years later in 2009). Throughout, I have experienced

Before she was stricken with a debilitating chronic illness, Debra McNie was a professional dancer.

emotions ranging from anger, denial, "why me," and "oh poor me," not productive for my ability to accept and adapt to being a woman living with chronic illness.

My self-esteem plummeted to such low depths, I couldn't recognize myself, nor did I want to. Former master at the helm of my ship, I was reduced to a sightseer. At first my relationships with friends and family were affected due to pride and my not wanting people to see "what I have become." Pride can be such a strong force. Intimate relations were challenged when I gained seventy pounds from medication, which contributed towards a very damaged self-image. I am truly blessed to have a life partner who has unconditionally taken this journey with me, and to have very supportive family, friends and one very tenacious family doctor. My gratitude for them is boundless.

Sometimes I do not appear ill, and well-intentioned people will remark on how well I am looking. I smile and say thank you, knowing I have just spent several days without sleep and have had to take narcotics to deal with pain. Beginning this journey, I felt left behind, observing my friends and family enjoying their days filled with school, work or other activities. Weekends once filled with entertaining friends, family activities or recreational sports, were now reduced to watching TV or maybe a coffee out. I have shed many tears shared only with the family pet. Moments of solitude often leave me to ponder if I will ever be well again. Sometimes I feel the need to explain, apologize and cover up for my illness. I often believed I was the only person experiencing this and as a result reached out to people less and isolated myself more.

To avoid writing the next great novel, I will make little mention of the endless consultations, paperwork and justifications for disability insurance, and the many hours spent in waiting rooms to see one specialist after another. Five years ago, I was at a comfortable point in my life and had no idea this path of discovery would force me to develop other aspects of my personality I might not have otherwise. In order to remain connected I had to be receptive to new places and people when I could no longer work or teach dance. I had to nurture what my life's path now was, and stop mourning what wasn't. Not being able to rely so heavily on my natural physical abilities, high energy level and leadership qualities, forced me to encourage the Debra who was yet to emerge. Mostly I had to start lifting the darkness and accept being ill and get on with my life.

I have learned that although I have limits, I am not limited; that the boundaries set upon me exist only because of my own fears and assumptions. Starting the healing process from within with the power of positive thinking, knowledge and prayer, has helped

"For a period I grieved the loss of my former self."

— DEBRA MCNIE

me to be more responsible for my own health and well-being. I began to take an active role in decisions regarding my health. Trying to eliminate stressful situations and people from my life was a difficult but necessary step. I can see I am not less than, but better for the experience of being ill. I have begun to let go of the past, and try to live in the present and trust I will have a future. I have learned to be more tolerant, patient and accepting of others, but mostly of myself. I am grateful for what I have, and I try not to dwell on what I don't have. True friendships have been instrumental in my ability to stay connected and reflective. I have learned the amazing power of a hug. I am trying to greet each day as it happens, good or bad. With all my faults and strengths I know that along with others, I am unique. Learning to love and be kind to myself, I believe, is instrumental in my ability to heal. This learning is a work in progress.

Having strong supportive friends, family and community has played a vital role in my ability to accept and adapt to being ill. Knowing without question I could just talk to someone has been very comforting. I have experienced a tremendous amount of loss, not only of my health, but also my ability to work, and to teach dance. For over thirty years, dance was a major part of my life as a profession and also as a vital creative outlet. Perhaps this was the greatest loss because so much of my self-esteem and self-worth and productiveness was wrapped up in my life as a dancer/teacher. For a period I grieved the loss of my former self, for I could no longer teach dance, work or go on hikes with my children. This journey has been a challenging and relentless one, with financial, emotional, physical, spiritual and mental setbacks.

Chronic illness had a tremendous impact on my status as a wife, mother, sister, daughter, friend and co-worker. My ability to function at the level I once did is diminished greatly. My sense of belonging decreased and my productiveness with work, community, and family, slowly dwindled to almost no involvement. My children often become confused, not knowing how to respond, help or relate to me. One day my heart rate dropped down to nineteen beats a minute. The decision was made to fly me to UBC Hospital research department. My children watched the ambulance attendants put me in the jet and fly away, not knowing whether they would ever see me again.

Debra McNie high-kicks a dance move in the great outdoors.

I have determined there is no one answer when trying to live with chronic illness. It takes an enormous amount of energy, information, responsibility and tenacity to be well. A healthy balance among mind, body, spirit and emotions is essential for everyone, but especially for a woman living with chronic illness. Accepting that I am ill has been a powerful catapult towards my ability to get on with life. Adapting to being ill has helped me to work towards putting strategies in place, and to be an active participant in my well-being. I encourage any woman who is ill and able, to explore as many avenues as possible, such as alternative medicines, acupuncture, massage, visualization, yoga, dance and meditation. Take charge of your health plan as this may be the greatest challenge of your life, and one which will require immense commitment and inner strength. I struggle daily to hang on to a sense of self and well-being. For me to remain connected, productive, involved and positive requires a great amount of energy. Volunteer work has helped me to fulfill that need and desire. For the most part I do well, but I long to feel like my old self again, even if just for a moment. Chronic illness remains an unpredictable and very formidable foe.

During the early hours of the night when I can't sleep I have been communicating online with other women who are chronically ill. This has helped me reflect, investigate and exchange ideas, and has given me the gift of understanding friendships with people I might never have met otherwise.

While I may not be who I once was, I am trying to be the best I can be. To quote a famous song, "You never know what you've got 'til it's gone!"

EDITOR'S NOTE

First published in *Interior Women's Magazine*, 1998.

Diane Walters

I don't think when you are living through difficult times that you think of yourself as overcoming adversity. So it is with hindsight that I look back on a portion of my life when everything was geared towards "partying on."

I didn't know at the time that I was living through an interesting period of history. Everything was a game in my life. Even getting married and moving away from small town BC to Jacksonville, Florida. My husband was in the American Air Force, and Jacksonville was where we were stationed when he left his overseas duty here in Canada.

It was during my time there that the small-town girl in me was overwhelmed by the differences in the two cultures. I saw and heard Martin Luther King speak. I watched demonstrations on the right to vote. I saw when the black population wanted to swim at a public beach, and how moms and dads and kids were turned back by the Troopers' dogs. Imagine what it was like when swimming in the ocean wasn't free for everyone. The emphatic distinction between black and white was very new for me. I spoke up as only an innocent outsider would and "partied on." Through my connection with the military I also got to see its ugly underbelly. I had more than my fair share of blissful ignorance regarding the Vietnam conflict; it never was a war! As such, I spouted off and partied on.

The one event of my life down south that will stand out forever was when I went into labour the day John F. Kennedy was assassinated. I couldn't believe that on a bright, sunny day in an open car, greeting his fellow Americans, the leader of this country was shot down for the entire world to see. Believe me, that was a tacky time to be on a military base. Everyone had to stay at their post, no one was to leave base, and so the doctors and nurses had to stay in the hospitals for what turned out to be days, and my premature labour just chugged along taking forever until I finally gave birth to a little boy. Three days later I was allowed to go home and believe me, did I ever party on.

Needless to say I was slowly but surely destroying my marriage. It wasn't until I had left my husband that I found myself on that slippery slope of not being fully responsible for my actions. I tried to kid myself that I had a handle on it, and it wasn't until I misplaced my son that I decided I'd better get my butt back to Canada and my family. I had decided to go partying one night and had taken Shaun to a house to be minded. The only thing was, when I sobered up I couldn't remember where it was that I took him. In the largest city in the state, and knowing very few people, I was fortunate to find the person who drove me to the babysitter's. Wow, that called for a drink, and so I partied on.

I came home to Canada shortly after that incident as I realized we would both not only be better off, but also safer back home. I then did what I think many of us who are so wrapped up in ourselves do; I turned myself and my son over to my family. No more worries.

How wrong I was, let me tell you. My folks were the most loving and caring people I have ever known. I never knew a day in my life when I wasn't the best thing since sliced bread in their eyes. I was always told how special I was and how much I was loved. Did I let that stand in my way? Never. I partied on.

Then after about a year of truly irresponsible behaviour, including a very severe auto accident which I caused, my family took drastic steps. There are defining moments in your life that will stay with you always. This was one of those times. Late one Sunday my folks were going out. They said that when they returned, they wanted us to be gone. I wasn't to call, come around, or have anything to do with them. I'd chosen my path and they weren't on it! It was beginning to be hard to party on.

I'd found some terrible little place for us to live, which was out of town, and I was without a car. Every morning we'd be on the road by 7 a.m. hitchhiking to get to my babysitter's and then I'd walk to my boss's house and he'd give me a ride in to work.

Luckily for me I worked at a place where there were a couple of fellows who went to AA (Alcoholics Anonymous). Every time I showed up for work rather hung down they would make fun of me and kept telling me they were saving a place for me at the meetings. After one particularly ugly night of partying, I asked to go to my first AA meeting. Here I was already washed up. I'd married by twenty-one; became a mother at twenty-three and was divorced at twenty-five. Now just after I celebrated my twenty-sixth birthday I was venturing down a road I surely didn't want to take.

I believe if I had known some of the hardships that lay ahead I may not have gone so willingly. Yet like so many things in the 1960s, everything was not as it seemed. Though the program claimed to be a fellowship of men and women, it really wasn't. At least not for a divorced, single parent woman of twenty-six. They all thought I wasn't taking the program seriously enough.

Somehow I managed to tough it out and finally got through that first year of sobriety. What a red-letter day that was for me. By this time my family had welcomed me back into the fold. Those early days were a challenge, as all those people I had once known kept their distance. I had either embarrassed them, used them in some fashion, or hurt them deeply. I had done many dreadful things, including writing cheques that couldn't clear the bank just so I could party on. What a day that was, going to the various stores and speaking to the managers about holding those rubber cheques and promising to pay all of my debts.

I kept my job until everyone was paid, and then I applied for a better job with better pay at my workplace. I worked for a steel company with its head office in Montreal, and those narrow-minded executives thought it wouldn't promote a good corporate image to have a woman selling steel. Good grief, I even trained the guy that got the job! Their rationale was that he had a family to support. What were my son and I, chopped liver?

Anyway, that became my year of getting to know my son after quitting my job on principle. I took that chance to learn how to be a parent. My poor son didn't really know me. I was just a swinging door to him.

At that time I wasn't aware of the equal rights movement, and they hadn't yet coined women's lib. I had been raised to believe that I was better than no one, but that I was equal to everyone. I was beginning to learn first-hand about double standards. All my life I had thought that kind of inequality only existed in the States, and so it came as a surprise to learn it happened right there in Kamloops, small town BC.

The same things happened in my AA meetings. It was as if you had to prove yourself to be qualified. Then just when it seemed I'd gotten a handle on my situation I was offered a job in Williams Lake. I had been out of work for a year. I needed desperately to make some money. I can't express the dread I felt of coming to an even smaller town and starting anew. But come we did.

I'll never forget that first night at a Williams Lake AA meeting. There were six of us there, and the guys were even glad to meet me. Little did I know at the time that the group was so small they just couldn't afford to be picky about who showed up.

The group started to grow and eventually some of the new members didn't like having me show up at meetings. I have yet to figure out why. One night at a meeting, I was told I shouldn't be allowed to come anymore. That was so against what the program stood for, I was thunderstruck. I remember walking out that evening absolutely broken-hearted, resolving to never set foot in a meeting again. But before I had a chance to leave, a fellow who had attended for many more years than I had, grabbed me by the arm and said, "Diane, I never thought I'd see the day when you'd let someone beat you down." You know when he put it like that I just couldn't quit. I'd show up if for no other reason than to drive them nuts.

One day I was visited at work by the fire chief, who told me that my house had burned down. At first I was devastated. Shaun and I didn't have a change of underclothes, never mind clothes, and we didn't have so much as a toothbrush. I remember going to the store to get those small necessities. All the while I never once thought about how a drink would go down well just then.

People were helpful, generous, and downright friendly in this small town. They truly typified the kind of people living in the Cariboo. One thing that always stood out for me was when someone donated a sewing box. Filled with thread, scissors, needles, buttons, and odds and ends; it was something so completely normal, handy, and useful. I try to remember that when a fire strikes another family, to send a sewing kit.

Just prior to the fire I had wanted to buy a car. I'll always remember the bank manager saying to me, "Good God, woman, you're a single parent, divorced and an alcoholic, what poorer risk could there be?" You see, in small town BC if you should happen to be someone like myself, one of the few women who actually went to AA and stayed, you became an oddity.

Nevertheless I have continued to be an active member in my sobriety community and in the community as a whole. It is important to give back more than you have received in all facets of life. Somehow since 1966 when I first embarked on a new path in life, the alternative to not changing my life around really wasn't an option. I worked hard to change what I could change, and learned I could be responsible for whatever or whoever came into my life. Self-confidence, pride, humility, and serenity are but the tip of the payoff earned in taking control of yourself. I wouldn't have it any other way. I was self-conscious at first to write about my life, but it isn't over yet. There are many more challenges to come. I can hardly wait.

Marilyn Berwin

BY SAGE BIRCHWATER

Marilyn Berwin has a spectacular view of the Coast Mountains from her tiny cabin in the West Chilcotin community of Tatla Lake. She's at home there with her two dogs, her painting easel, and comfy artist's studio. Nearby, in two locations, at Tatla Lake Christian Fellowship Church, and in West Chilcotin Trading general store, the bulk of her oil paintings on canvas, hardboard and recycled circular saw blades are on display. For the most part Marilyn is a self-taught landscape artist.

She was born in 1942 in the remote sawmill town of Penny, east of Prince George, where her father was a sawmill worker. She was the oldest girl of seven children.

"I had one older brother and the rest were girls," she says. "I grew up in Penny until I was twelve years old. My parents didn't want their girls to stay in the Prince George dorm, so we moved to Kamloops where I graduated from high school."

Kamloops was the largest city in the British Columbia interior in the mid-1950s.

"I don't do town," Marilyn confesses. "I'm a bush rat. That's all there is to it."

She says her childhood dreams involved horses, and from early on she drew and sketched them. It would be years before she ever owned one.

"I don't do town... I'm a bush rat."

— MARILYN BERWIN

"I wanted to major in art," she says. "But when I got to grade ten my parents told me getting a fine arts degree wouldn't get you a job."

So she relished every second of the two years she was able to take art classes in high school.

"I started painting some in high school. I always loved to paint and draw horses. Then I took secretarial and just developed my own thing as far as artwork goes, from then on."

When she was fifteen years old Marilyn met her future husband, Bill Berwin. He was a tall, quiet young man who came to Kamloops to work in a sawmill. Bill boarded with Lou Haynes in the Mission Flats sawmilling community where Marilyn and her family lived.

"I met him in Kamloops but I wouldn't talk to him as he seemed older than my other teen friends."

Then Marilyn and a girlfriend double dated. Her girlfriend dated Bill and Marilyn dated another fellow. She says the more they were around each other, the more she and Bill took a shine to each other.

"What sold me on him, he had this picture in his wallet of himself and a blaze-faced sorrel. Bill was all duded up in western gear. He was one sexy-looking cowboy."

Tragedy struck Marilyn's family when her dad was killed in a sawmillng accident when she was in grade eleven. The following year she missed most of her final year of high school due to medical problems and grieving the loss of her father.

"I only went to school four months in grade twelve."

She still managed to graduate from high school, and a year later in 1961, at the age of eighteen, Marilyn and Bill Berwin got married. They honeymooned on the top of the Potato Mountains in the Chilcotin, and for a wedding present, Harry Haynes, who was like an uncle to Bill, gave the couple ten acres of land in Tatlayoko Valley. In 1963 Bill built an eighteen-by-twenty-four-foot log cabin there for the couple to live in. When they moved out to Tatlayoko, Bill went to work logging. He eventually got hired on as a sawyer at the new Lignum sawmill on Tatlayoko Lake.

Life unfolded for the young couple in the Chilcotin, with the birth of their two children, Bonnie (1963) and Danny (1968), and they soon got into ranching, getting an agricultural pre-emption a kilometre or so up the hillside from their ten acres near Skinner Mountain.

"It was the very last pre-emption let out by the government," Marilyn says. "In five years we had 1,200 square bales of hay coming off the deeded eighty-acre area."

In 1974, Bill and Marilyn signed the papers to buy Harry Haynes' ranch, and the ink was barely dry when the Lignum sawmill burned to the ground. Overnight the Berwins were without a dependable income.

"When the mill burned down Bill went away to work every winter for five years in the Silvacan mill in Takla Landing," Marilyn says.

That left her to run the ranch on her own and to look after their two children and manage one hundred head of cattle.

"It was a challenge," she says. "There were no proper corrals to contain the cattle, the septic system was broken, the well was filled with mud, and there was no electricity. Every winter the gravity water line froze so water had to be hauled for the stock by team and sleigh."

Marilyn found it difficult running the ranch on her own while Bill was away and she got very depressed.

"When Billy was out working, he couldn't get a concept of what it was like for me being there by myself. There was no calving barn, no running water, no indoor plumbing. Those things really depressed me."

Then one night, alone in her cabin in January 1980, in a state of despair, Marilyn had a profound religious experience that changed her whole outlook on life.

"I was born again, and that experience carried me through," she says.

But she says her religious conversion caused a rift between herself and her husband.

"Me being a Christian put a wall between us. After I got saved I wanted to get close to God without making waves in our relationship."

But she says that wasn't easy.

"It wasn't fun for me to go to dances any longer with all the partying and drinking. It caused a schism between me and Billy. He was really struggling. It was like spiritual warfare."

Then on June 19, 1982, tragedy struck.

Marilyn, Bill and Danny were moving cattle down the west side of Tatlayoko Lake to summer range, and they had to drive the herd across Jamison Creek, which was a torrent of white water fed by the spring snow melt from the alpine area above.

Bill was positioned on his horse where the creek flowed into the lake as they coaxed the cows and calves through the current. Then his horse lost his footing as one back foot slipped off the sharp drop-off where the riverbed met the lake, and the horse plunged into the deep water, breaking its front saddle cinch and throwing Bill into the frigid water.

Bill couldn't swim and the current of the creek carried him further and further from shore. Marilyn says she felt helpless. As she and Danny searched the nearby forest for a long pole or a chunk of wood they could float out to Bill, she noticed his bobbing head disappear from sight. That's when Marilyn says she fell to her knees and cried out: "God save him!"

"I felt great peace like when I was saved two years earlier," she says. "The cops came out later that day and I gave a statement, then the next day they came out again with a dive team and found Bill's body."

Marilyn says the senior RCMP officer sat down with her and told her there was something she needed to know. "Most people who drown," he said, "show evidence that they fought it. There's usually evidence that their death was difficult, that the body went through agony."

But in Bill's case, when the dive team found his body in eighty feet of water, a hundred feet from shore, he said the divers were surprised to find him laying on his back with his hands folded on his chest.

"He had a totally peaceful look on his face, the cop told me."

That was the most important thing for Marilyn, who felt her cry out to God was answered.

After twenty-one years of marriage, at the age of thirty-nine, Marilyn was now a widow. Danny was only fourteen and Bonnie was nineteen, finishing her second year of agricultural college. Rather than sell the ranch and move away, Marilyn and the kids decided to stick with it, at least for the rest of that summer and fall. With the help of her children Marilyn continued ranching and started fixing things up.

"The year that Bill died we had to rebuild all the corrals, and put in the septic system. Lyman Thompson from Kleena Kleene Ranch got a work bee together and they put a roof on the newly built calving barn."

Two years after Billy died, Marilyn had an electric branding iron, a calving barn with electricity, a new concrete root cellar, and running water.

"Branding was easy, calving was easy. I thought, oh man, this was so much pleasanter. But it could have come sooner. Bill was a stubborn, typical-Chilcotin cowboy with romantic, outdated notions of how to operate a ranch. There was women's work and guy work. But Bill refused to share in the women's work."

She says Bill was an awesome mechanic and was great with horses, but he had no idea how hard it was for her to run the ranch on her own. Especially calving all those years he worked out at Silvacan.

Marilyn says within two years after Bill died, she managed to transform the place from a four-person haywire, labour-intensive show into a one-woman ranch that was more streamlined and ran easily.

She says there were a lot of people involved who helped make the transformation of the ranch possible.

"But I had the vision to see what was needed, and experience to alleviate problems where possible."

In 1986, with the ranch running smoother, Marilyn sold the property and moved out of the Chilcotin for thirteen years. She would return every year for visits, then in 1999 she moved back to the Chilcotin for good.

Throughout her married life Marilyn managed to find time for her artwork during the long Chilcotin winters, amassing a fair collection of oil paintings of landscapes and horses and wildlife. After returning to the Chilcotin in 1999, she moved into a small cabin near Tatla Lake. With fewer demands on her table, she could paint throughout the year whenever the spirit moved her.

Marilyn Berwin paints in her studio near Tatla Lake where she creates beautiful landscapes in oils and acrylics.

"When the inspiration comes, I drop everything," Marilyn confesses. "I love the remoteness of the Chilcotin. It inspires me. I love the fall colours."

She says one of her favourite paintings of swans flying over Hook Lake was purchased by Tatlayoko ranchers Charlie and Ruth Travers last fall.

"Ruth and Charlie are birders and they really liked it," she says. "The painting was only hanging in the church for three weeks before the Travers bought it."

Marilyn says she goes out into nature on her four-wheeler, packing her camera and taking photos of the landscapes she wants to paint.

"I never paint from one photo. It's usually a composite."

Marilyn says she developed her own painting style over the years without formal instruction.

"I think my style has improved a little bit over the years," she says. "Mostly by doing."

EDITOR'S NOTE:
This article appeared in *Casual Country*, 2009.

Audrey MacLise

AUTOBIOGRAPHY

I first saw the light of day at Nurse LePage's Hospital in Fort Saskatchewan, Alberta, in 1929 where my maternal grandparents, Jack and Margaret Karran, were early pioneers. I was born during the Great Depression, and was the youngest of four children in the household. My parents, Preston and Emily Bugden, were both active community supporters who involved their children in everything they did.

My father was employed as a station agent for the Northern Alberta Railway, putting his family in a better position than many during the early years of the Depression. Being the youngest child had some advantages; the main one was that I was allowed to be my father's little tag-along when the other children were in school and mother was busy doing what mothers do.

The best memories were made when I could ride up the track with Dad on the pump speeder to the elevators where Dad would check with the elevator agents to see how many grain cars they would need each week. The agents were always happy to see us, but my favourite agent was Ernie Jones, because he was always generous with his bag of peppermints! On another of the trips we drove over to the Penn Coal Mine in Carbondale to check with the foreman regarding his need for railway cars. We often had to go down the main shaft in a makeshift elevator to locate the foreman. We did not use hard hats in those days; the miners just wore caps with a light attached to the front. My mother always admonished me that I was not to go into the mine, but how could I pass up such a great opportunity, and I knew Dad would give in if I coaxed. I did not like Mrs. Baerge, the mine owner, after we discovered that the mine's agreement stated she was to provide each miner with a lunch when they came on shift, but all they got was two slices of bread with a slab of lard in between. There was no shop steward to complain to then.

When it was time for school, I attended a two-room country school four miles away. In the summer we walked the distance, but in winter Dad hired a farmer's son to drive us in a sleigh. Although we were only twenty miles from Edmonton, the roads were not often ploughed for vehicular traffic. In time, my father was able to convince the Department of Education to build a one-room school in our community so the miners' children could attend school regularly. The teacher who was hired was quite young and had difficulty controlling the class. Some of the boys were fifteen or sixteen and in grades four or five, so my father would often come to the school and sit at the back of the room reading. Mother learned Morse code so she could record messages that came in over the telegraph when my father had to be out. It was not long until Dad and Mother also had a Sunday school up and running in the school building.

In 1937, we quickly learned the harsh realities of life when we lost our beloved father to a massive heart attack at the young age of thirty-six. Our family had to move out of the station to allow a new agent to move in. My grandparents, who had raised ten children, were now alone, and they welcomed us into their home. I was happy in my grandparents' home, but unfortunately there was very little work for women in Fort Saskatchewan. After a year, we moved to Edmonton where Mother could find part-time work in the schools. Money was always in short supply, but everyone seemed to be in the same situation so we did not feel disadvantaged. We soon learned to take little jobs to help with finances at home. When in high school, I was very pleased to land a job in a fine ladies' wear store, where I worked Saturdays and holidays. This was, without a doubt, where I developed my appreciation for fashion.

After graduation, I attended McTavish Business College in Edmonton where I found accounting to be my niche. On graduating from McTavish, I was fortunate enough to secure a position in the Department of Municipal Affairs with the Alberta government. To apply for this job, I arrived suitably attired in a tailored business dress, small hat, and gloves, only to find I had to stand in line with about eighteen others to even get an interview.

Eventually my superior encouraged me to take cost accounting courses being offered through the University of Alberta. These courses eventually led me to take a job with the Flint Rig Company. The oil boom had just hit Edmonton and jobs in this field were paying well. Flint Rig was a drilling company that had been in business for thirty-five years with offices in Texas, Oklahoma, and Venezuela but had never had a female employee. I soon discovered I was not only the branch accountant but also the entertainment.

One day the manager told me there was a green Chevy out in the pipe yard that I could have the use of if I got a driver's licence. It did not take me long to take a few driving lessons and get a driver's licence. The manger gave me the keys and told me I would probably have to back the car out of the pipe yard. When I walked down to the car, I discovered it was parked between two long stacks of drill pipe, and if I were to back into one of those pipes the whole stack would probably fall down on me. Needless to say, I backed out of there very, very slowly. When I got to the end and started to turn out, I looked up to the office windows only to see the entire staff standing laughing and clapping. I knew it was a set-up. This prank was just one of many they played on me over the next three years.

My next job was with Imperial Oil in Calgary as the cost accountant in the production department. This was a great company to work for; they paid well and everyone received a good bonus at year's end. The company struck oil in the Peace River country and thirty-five people from the Calgary office were asked to transfer to Peace River to open a production office. I went willingly as it was a step up for me, and my mother and stepfather were living at Grimshaw, just seventeen miles away. At Imperial Oil, our staff formed our own social club, funded by Imperial Oil. We hosted many social events and invited the townspeople to come and join us. This made us all very welcome in the town of Peace River.

On July 1, 1954, my friend Nora and I accompanied my parents to a sports day dance at Bear Lake Pavillion just beyond Grimshaw. Soon after arriving at the dance, my mother introduced Nora and me to Bill Dixon and Hugh MacLise. Nora and Bill were married in April 1955 and Hugh and I married in May 1955. Nora and I stood up at each other's wedding.

Hugh and I bought a house in Grimshaw and proceeded to renovate it. Our son, Scot, was born in 1956. Hugh worked very long hours as pharmacist in the drugstore, and after three winters he subsequently bought a partnership in a drugstore in Vermilion, Alberta, in 1958. While in Vermilion, our daughter, Alison, was born. Vermilion was a pretty, well-established community but the winters were still long. This prompted us to sell this partnership and move to Penticton in July 1961. We had discovered the warmer climate in Pentiction while visiting Hugh's family in the Okanagan Valley.

We enjoyed Penticton for just one year while Hugh searched the Okanagan Valley for a viable business opportunity. In July 1962, we journeyed to Williams Lake to look at Cunningham Drugs, which was coming up for sale as the manager wished to retire soon. We loved Penticton, but found the business climate was unsure as the city was more or less supported by the tourist trade in summer. Hugh felt the business possibilities in Williams Lake would be year-round so on August 23, 1962, we moved to Williams Lake. Hugh was owner/manager of Cunningham Drugs until he sold to Shopper's Drug Mart in 1976.

This fourteen-year period was a positive time for our young family. Scot and Alison settled into school and did well with many dedicated teachers. I became a hockey, figure skating, and swimming mom and served on the hospital auxiliary, hospital board and Cariboo Festival Society Board. My work on the hospital board led me to serve on the building committee for the Nurses Residence and the Cariboo Park Home for seniors.

"I became a hockey, figure skating, and swimming mom..."

— AUDREY MACLISE

In 1966, we had a new home built for us in a new subdivision on the edge of town. We settled into our new home on a well-wooded lot on Boitanio Street and watched the neighbourhood grow up around us. In 1968, we purchased a large, treed lot with a small, rustic cabin on Chimney Lake. This treasured spot became the location of choice for all family parties and get-togethers and remains so to this day. At this time the road from Williams Lake to Chimney Lake was a rough gravelled road, so whenever it started to rain we had to either head for home immediately or decide to stay for at least three days until the road was fit to travel over again.

A holiday tradition began at this time when several couples who had property on the lake got together at Ringwood's cabin each Wrestling Day (January 2, the day after New Year's Day). We bundled up, took our children along, and walked across the frozen lake to the Poole home where we were served mulled wine to warm us before we trekked back to Ringwood's for our hot potluck dinner. What a wonderful way to end the Holiday season.

After both children were in school I took a job as accountant with the local newspaper and after working for approximately one year as office manager, the publisher asked me to move to the advertising department and take over the job of advertising manager. I had helped in that department and enjoyed the challenges of selling the product; however there was a catch. I knew the job of advertising manager would be more demanding and time consuming than the job I was doing so I asked for the same salary that the then advertising manager was receiving. The publisher told me in no uncertain terms that I would have to remain at the salary I was getting as office manager because my husband was earning good money as a pharmacist and I did not need a higher salary. Unfortunately, this was the thinking of the day. In response to this rather definite statement, I said I thought the company should pay whatever the job was worth whether it was a man or a woman who filled the position. I stated that if they were not prepared to do this I would prefer to remain in my job as office manager and not take on the additional responsibility. The discussion went back and forth for a week and then the publisher decided I was quite stubborn and he agreed to the higher salary. I continued in this job for two years then felt it was time for a change as the hours were much too long.

The following year, I taught Accounting I and II for Cariboo College Continuing Education. I really enjoyed teaching adults two evenings a week. During the day, I took the real

Audrey MacLise, left, with Williams Lake Mayor Kerry Cook. PHOTO KAREN LONGWELL

estate salesman's course by correspondence from the Faculty of Commerce at UBC and attained my real estate salesman's licence in 1971. I went to work as a saleslady for the first Williams Lake Realty. After two years I took the real estate agent's course through the Faculty of Commerce at UBC, again by correspondence. This was a year-long course and at times quite onerous while working full-time and caring for my family.

After securing my real estate agent's licence I opened my own business, MacLise Realty, in 1975. I became the first female real estate agent in Williams Lake. My previous agent told me I was a foolish woman and he would run me out of business in six months. However, MacLise Realty thrived and prospered and as my children were teenagers by this time, and anxious for part-time jobs, I involved them as much as I could. In all, I was an active realtor for twenty-seven years; many of my clients became my friends, as did many of my competitors. During my real estate career, I served two two-year terms as a director on the Cariboo Real Estate Board.

In 1977, my husband decided he too would like a career change, so he took the real estate salesman's course and joined me at MacLise Realty. Hugh just wanted to sell land and the freedom this prospect offered him. After twenty-five years of long hours in a pharmacy this held a lot of appeal for him. He already knew many of the country folk in this area and so enjoyed serving them in a different way.

The real estate industry nationally went through a rough episode beginning in 1982 when interest rates soared to eighteen percent and gradually ended in 1985 as interest rates declined. In 1982, there were five real estate offices in Williams Lake. By 1985, there was only Realty World Northern and MacLise Realty still in business.

Unfortunately, Hugh was diagnosed with Alzheimer's disease in the 1980s. He was only fifty-eight years old at the time and so was considered early-onset. Very little information or community services were available for family caregivers at that time. My doctor advised me to keep on working if I could. Through a mutual friend, I was able to hire a competent caregiver to live with us and care for Hugh when I was at work. In 1989, we had to place Hugh in a care facility. I spent a year on the road visiting him on weekends first in Vancouver and then in Kamloops. It was during this time I realized the daily stress was taking a toll on both my family and me. Our children had both finished university and our son Scot was married in 1986. In 1990, I closed MacLise Realty and went to work for ReMax, then Realty World Northern.

In January 1990, I found I was receiving a growing number of calls from families who had a family member who had been diagnosed with Alzheimer's disease or a related dementia. I had spoken to the Alzheimer Society on several occasions and they had suggested I start an Alzheimer support group in Williams Lake. For the past nineteen years I have been the local facilitator for the Alzheimer Society. I have attended many seminars and workshops in this field, and in 2002 I was instrumental in the development of the Adult Day Centre in Williams Lake.

In June 2007 a group of volunteers and I decided to open an Alzheimer Resource Centre located in the Seniors' Activity Centre in Williams Lake. We hold our support group meetings there and are open two days a week to the general public.

November 1995 brought the birth of our granddaughter Emily, and although she now lives in another community, I am able to attend her special occasions. At the moment, these occasions are mainly dance recitals and festivals for song and verse.

Hugh passed away peacefully in June 1998, ending his long and courageous battle with Alzheimer's disease. It was our battle too, and it taught our family tolerance, humility, compassion, and above all, endurance.

In September 1998, I was appointed to the Seniors' Advisory Council of BC for a three-year term. This opportunity encouraged me to take my retirement from real estate in December 1998. As a member of the Seniors' Advisory Council, I gained extensive experience working with community groups throughout the province. The other representatives on the council were very experienced, knowledgeable and interesting and I became good friends with several of the others on the committee. As part of this council, I coordinated the development of a report entitled *A Social Support Strategy for Enhancing the Quality of Life of Individuals with Dementia*. To date, the Ministry of Health has not yet developed a positive strategy for caring for dementia patients.

In July 2002, I had the opportunity to gather four other interested people to travel to Prince George and attend a workshop on "How to Begin an Elder College." By the time we returned to Williams Lake we had formed a steering committee to take on this exciting challenge. In January 2003, Cariboo Chilcotin Elder College was able to present our first semester of four academic courses and four computer courses through Thompson Rivers University. Elder College is an idea whose time has come with a wonderful response from the community and a growing number of local instructors. I have had the privilege of acting as chair of Cariboo Chilcotin Elder College since we began in 2002.

I am also currently founder and chair of the Seniors' Advisory Council of Williams Lake and area. A member of the BC Regional Review Committee for New Horizons Seniors Programs, the Community Response Network, and Social Planning Advisory Network.

I view retirement as that small window of opportunity given us near the end of our journey to use the skills we have acquired along the way. It has been quite easy for me to see some of the needs in our own community for I have indeed lived in "interesting times." My motto is "never stagnate—continue to grow and learn to articulate your feelings when it's necessary to do so."

Sarah-Spring Stump

BY SAGE BIRCHWATER
WITH LUANNE BEST, DANNY STUMP & MAUREEN TICKNER

Sarah-Spring Stump has often been called a saint in Williams Lake because she lived her life as Mother Theresa did, taking into her home the destitute and homeless. Most of these high-risk street alcoholics were aboriginal, but not all of them. Sarah was very inclusive about accepting everybody. "Mom never categorized anyone," says her oldest daughter, Luanne Best. "She opened her doors for whites and natives alike, to aboriginals of all tribes. To all tribes, Mom was the same."

Born on July 7, 1940, in Edmonton, Alberta, Sarah passed away at sixty-eight in Williams Lake on February 23, 2009. She left behind a legacy of helping others. She also left behind Abraham's Lodge, the home she established with her husband, Danny Stump, which continues to give refuge to people down on their luck. If it weren't for Sarah, many people, including Danny himself, would not be alive today.

Since she was a young child, Sarah lived her life by faith. She was the third-oldest of seventeen children born to Nona and Ervin Combs of Rocky Rapids, Alberta. Her family was devoutly religious, and her father, Ervin Leander Combs, was a Baptist minister in Rocky Rapids, a community of 300 people southwest of Edmonton where his parents pioneered. On her mother's side, Sarah was Metis and a direct descendant of Alexander Mackenzie, the Scottish explorer who crossed North America by land in 1793. Mackenzie

Sarah-Spring Stump is being congratulated by Prime Minister Jean Chrétien when she was presented with the Governor General's Caring Canadian Award in Ottawa in June, 2001.

was her great-great-grandfather.

When she was seventeen, Sarah gave birth to Luanne out of wedlock. Then she married and had two more children, Nola and Calvin. After an abusive marriage, she eventually divorced her husband.

Maureen Tickner first met Sarah in 1983 at a care-aid program Maureen was giving at Cariboo College in Williams Lake for mature women coming into the workforce. In a sharing circle Maureen asked the students what they had done previously, and says she was blown away when Sarah told the group she had been a housewife, a logging truck driver, and had a gold claim before badly hurting her back.

"I liked her right away," says Maureen. "She was a very unique, powerful and strong woman with a big heart. She had a deep, deep religious belief to help others, doing God's work."

It was around this time that Sarah saw the street people diving into garbage bins scrounging for food to survive on, and when the weather got colder she invited them into her apartment to keep them from freezing. This led to Sarah getting evicted and moving into a larger apartment to continue her work helping the poor.

One of the street people Sarah helped was Danny Stump. He says when they met in 1987 he was a street drunk and his life was "kind of a blur." Then Danny and Sarah hit it off romantically and formed a lifelong partnership. They got married on June 10, 1987. "After we got married she asked me to give my heart to the Lord," Danny says. "So I did. One day I was a drunk and the next day was like I had never drank before in my life. I didn't quit drinking, I just didn't drink any more. I took the short cut and didn't even go to detox."

When Danny gave his heart to the Lord, Sarah anointed him with a gallon of pure virgin olive oil. "My black vest stained right through to my shirt," he says, describing his time with Sarah as twenty-two years of a wonderful life.

As a partnership, Sarah and Danny accomplished a lot. For a couple of years they set up a home for street people in the pastoral area of Soda Creek north of Williams Lake along the Fraser River, and involved them in farming and animal husbandry activities, driving back and forth picking up clients from the drunk tank and hospital. Then they formed Abraham's Lodge and Care Society, a non-profit society, and purchased a large home on the outskirts of Williams Lake at 505 Wotsky Drive and Hodgson Road. In the cold weather Sarah and Danny would go out and search for their street clients to bring them indoors and feed and clothe them. When taken in, the clients would be treated for their sickness, including hypothermia, lice, frostbite, scabies, parasites, etc. "We went looking for people under railway bridges," Danny says. "We'd find cardboard boxes with people sleeping in them."

Maureen Tickner marvels over what a great place Abraham's Lodge became and how Sarah and Danny managed to make it all work with virtually no financial support. "I never met anyone who could survive and live on a shoestring like that," Maureen says. "Sarah made it work. The boys (from the street) were her family. It was a miracle; amazing how it worked. They had up to twenty-five at the lodge at one time."

When she visted her mom in the beginning, Luanne says her house was always full. "Mom got kicked out of her apartment because she had fifty people staying with her there." Sarah's three children supported their mother and did not hold her accountable for missing any weddings, birthings or birthday celebrations because Sarah was helping others. Her children and grandchildren were there to help as volunteers too. Luanne remembers her mom asked for a vehicle to transport food, people and household items. "Mom asked: 'Lovie (the name she always called me) could you find a van and get me one?' The next day my husband, Jim, purchased a van and we drove it to the Lodge the next day." Though it was not new, Sarah and Danny put many miles on this vehicle and many other vehicles that were donated for the use of Abraham's Lodge and Care Society.

Danny says when they first started accommodating the street people they didn't impose any rules or conditions, but that soon changed. "The rules just popped up," Danny explains. Now the rules are basic. No drugs, no alcohol, no cussing, no congregating in one room. We leave one room open, so if you're stranded you can come in and crash."

"We went looking for people under railway bridges..."

— DANNY STUMP

Luanne says her mother imposed the same rules for Abraham Lodge that a loving mother would have. "If you're verbally abusive, there would be a consequence, like soap in the mouth for cussing, or down the road you went."

Now, Danny says, there's a core group of seven residents who live at Abraham's Lodge.

The True Volunteer

To be a true volunteer for your country is a wonderful way to express your love for your fellow mankind. The most rewarding feeling is to help another person in need without charge, right in your own community. All people of the world have a human need to be loved and respected no matter who they are, what they look like, colour, race, nationality, old or young, appealing and/or even frightening to us, we should try to see one another with eyes of kindness and respect.

It is true that pure love can make the world into a healthy community. If we all would take the time to consider the people around us without first consideration to ourselves and our own needs, rather reaching out to our fellow mankind with true compassion and willingness to serve and assist one another, surely this world would be a wonderful place to live.

— Sarah-Spring Stump

"The boys receive their mail there. They're proud of the lodge. They call it home."

Maureen says Sarah was continually at odds with government bureaucracies and the rules set out to govern social agencies. "She wanted to run it her way, not the government's way. She took in people who were drunk or high. It was the only place in town where there were no barriers. The government just wouldn't listen."

During the early years of the Society, Sarah went elsewhere for funds, appealing to the community, businesses and non-profit organizations like Help the Aged Canada. Safeway of Canada gave day-old bread. This was such a great help to those who were hungry. Sarah and Danny would deliver to the reserves all items donated to the Lodge. For many years Danny picked up donated items of food until September of 2008 when listeria was found in food. Safeway stopped donating after this notification to the public. This greatly affected the people who came to the food bank at Abraham's Lodge after that date.

Every year Sarah saw that the need for food during the winter was crucial so she came up with the idea of the Winter Circle of Sharing. This involved Rogers Foods donating a forty-foot van full of dried goods. Help the Aged paid for the transportation to Abraham's Lodge and out to all eighteen reserves that called for assistance.

That's one program that will continue despite the listeria scare and the passing of Sarah, assures Luanne. "Abraham's Lodge will continue with the Winter Circle of Sharing program with the continued support of Rogers Foods and Help the Aged Canada."

Sarah continued to profess her Christianity and reserved the right to counsel people

Sarah-Spring and Danny Stump are introduced to Governor General Adrienne Clarkson in June, 2001, when they were presented with the Governor General's Caring Canadian Award.

staying in the lodge according to her beliefs. "She believed her mission was to spread love that God gave her to hand out," Luanne says. "Mom never took any welfare but trusted in the Lord for everything she needed. She put up a sign, 'Jesus is Love,' on the main door. Before she died she said, don't you take down my sign."

Sarah's open stance on religion caused problems with the government that insisted her facility be secular, therefore making it difficult to obtain financial support.

Despite her unorthodox style, Sarah helped numerous people turn their lives around. Maureen Tickner says she witnessed one young man come back to the Lodge to thank Sarah one time. "She took him in and got him a job doing some construction work, then he got a job at Western Star before moving way up north. He married a woman who was a chief up there. Then ten years later he came back with his little girl driving a brand new truck. He knocked on the door of the Lodge, introduced his daughter to Sarah, and told Sarah he wanted to thank her."

Besides helping to accommodate the needs of the street people in Williams Lake, Danny and Sarah sent the food and clothing they collected out to eighteen reserves in the surrounding region from Sugar Cane, Esket, Dog Creek and Canoe Creek, all the way out to Ulkatcho in Anahim Lake in the West Chilcotin, Redstone, Stone, Anaham and Nemiah Valley, and to Nazko and Lhuzkus west of Quesnel. Plus many more reserves who called for assistance. Anything that is donated to the Lodge is freely given to anyone needing it, Danny says.

Sarah-Spring and Danny Stump with clients Alex Etienne and Herbert Setah.

Sarah and Danny have been recognized for their work locally, provincially and nationally. Sarah was nominated twice for the citizen of the year for Williams Lake (1993, 1995). In 2001 both Danny and Sarah were given the Governor General's Caring Canadian Award in Ottawa, and had dinner with Prince Charles and Prime Minister Jean Chrétien. In June 2001 Sarah was given the Order of British Columbia, and in 2002 she received the Queen's Golden Jubilee Medal. Also in 2002 Danny and Sarah were the honourary parade marshals for the Williams Lake Stampede parade.

Sarah was very musical, playing the piano, guitar, accordion, mouth organ and many other instruments. Her husband Danny is also very musical. In the fall of 2002, Danny, Sarah and family recorded and distributed the CD *I'm Not Homeless* to promote Abraham's Lodge and the work done there. The CD was made available to the public, with donations accepted.

Toward the end of her life Sarah was bed-ridden and confined to a wheelchair to get around, yet she still did her work directing the activities at Abraham's Lodge. Danny says she wore out her knees searching out the street people in their way-out places to bring them into shelter. "She had bad health problems," he says. "In 2003 we went to see a specialist doctor in California. Her knees were rubbing bone on bone." There was no treatment for her so Sarah carried on as usual, without complaining to anyone, just praying for her work to continue.

Luanne says her mother was always an advocate for those most unloved. "She always said the Lord must be uplifted. There was no glory for Sarah. It is difficult for anyone to understand what it's like to live on the streets unless they've done so themselves."

Besides the Lodge, Sarah leaves a legacy of writing—children's stories, songs, poems, and a book, *Star Wars of the Ages*, about Revelations. "She knew what was going to happen," says Luanne. "What's in her book is happening now," Danny adds.

Sarah was also director of the Eagle Wings Project in 2004. Maureen Tickner, Luanne Best, Ken Grant and Danny Stump were also directors. It was Sarah's dream for all the people in aboriginal communities to have

Sarah-Spring and Danny Stump in a warm embrace.

access to all medical health needs: hospitals, treatments, training schools, housing, ranching, gardens and pure drinking water. This project was guaranteed by private funds and approved by the directors. However, Sarah's failing health and being short-staffed at the Lodge makes it nearly impossible to get out west to the Chilcotin. "It seems there is a great divide between the outback and the interior," says Luanne. "Life is a struggle out west for those who live on the reserves."

Luanne says her mother was a true volunteer. "My mother's laughter was from her belly, and she cried right from the heart. It is a blessing to have had her as my mother, friend and confident. I miss her terribly but I know I must go on. My dad (Danny) and I and the directors of the Lodge will carry Mom's legacy."

Danny, Luanne, and the directors of Abraham's Lodge and Care Society will continue to help the needy and homeless of Williams Lake and surrounding area every day. "Though Sarah has gone, the work at Abraham's Lodge will continue," Danny insists. "As long as the Lord wills it."

Acknowledgements

This book would not have been possible without the determination and caring of many people. Special thanks are due to the women who shared their stories and to their family members and friends who helped in the process. Thanks also to the writers and researchers who helped bring these stories alive.

Thank you to Jenny DeReis who planned this project for the Women's Contact Centre, and to the staff and board members who helped with it: Basha Rahn, Erinn Brown, Judy Williams and Karen Kuenzl.

Irene Wilsey, director of the Women's Contact Centre used her organizational and fundraising skills to involve community and business groups in supporting and paying for the project.

Deep appreciation is due to the *Williams Lake Tribune* for use of photographs and permission to include articles previously published in the newspaper and yearly *Casual Country* supplement.

Thanks also to Pat Skoblanuik and the Museum of the Cariboo Chilcotin for cooperation in providing information and photographs.

This book would not have been possible without the editorial management of Sage Birchwater, and the drive and determination of advisory committee members Pam Mahon, Karen Thompson and Gloria Atamanenko who were responsible for keeping the project alive after it lay dormant for a few years.

Special thanks to Caitlin Press publisher, Vici Johnstone, who recognized the value of giving a voice to the women who have been the foundation of life in the Cariboo Chilcotin for the past century or more.